The GREENBRIER HERITAGE

by

William Olcott

Library of Congress
catalog card number
67-16176

DEDICATION

The Greenbrier Heritage is so much a story of people that it is to them this book is dedicated—To those who have served visitors to White Sulphur Springs for almost two centuries; And to The Greenbrier personnel of today, upon whose pride of service depends The Greenbrier Heritage of tomorrow.

Truman Wright

CONTENTS

A WALK THROUGH HISTORY

Stand at The Greenbrier's north portico in the softness
of a summer's night and the present merges into the past:
for once again, the ghosts of history come alive. Right in
front of you—within the formal gardens of today—stood
the west piazza of the historic hotel we remember as
The Old White.

Imagine you are back in the year 1867. Walk up the
steps to the wide veranda and peer through mullioned
windows. Candles by the hundreds, in crystal chandelier
and wall sconce, illuminate a splendid scene. As your eyes
adjust to the light, you can see the belles and beaux waiting
for the next dance to begin. And now, that mustached
Meyer Davis of an earlier day, Professor J. A.
Rosenberger, gives the signal and his Celebrated Brass
and String Band begins to play. A waltz, perhaps, or a
gavotte. It could even be an early version of "The
Original Lover's Leap Galop, a Scene from the Greenbrier
White Sulphur Springs," which Maestro Rosenberger is to
publish in 1871. As the dancers begin, the flickering
lights and blue shadows cast their spell, and you forget
the little flaws in the picture—the damask gown that had,
too obviously, been a drapery, the gray-suited dancer with
an empty sleeve. For the season at White Sulphur has begun.

A charming memoir of that summer was written by Miss Christiana Bond of Baltimore:

"Not only the legendary charms of the 'Springs' before the war allured us, but the expectation of meeting...the defeated wearers of the Gray...whom our enthusiasm invested with so many chivalric virtues. It is impossible for a girl of today [she wrote in 1926] to comprehend the romantic interest with which the heroes of the war were viewed by the girls of that time."

The hero of heroes is General Robert E. Lee. Miss Bond met him on the way to White Sulphur when he allowed her party to use a room reserved for the invalid Mrs. Lee. This friendship was to continue when they reached The White.

"Every evening General Lee marshalled a merry group of girls, and sat in the midst while partners came and went. He loved to see them taking part in their natural pleasures, but he guarded from urgency or ridicule the scrupulous one who looked wistfully on. For in those days there were not a few whose family training debarred them from the fun, or who joined only in the Lancers or the Virginia Reel, and wondered whether 'round' dances could really be so wrong. To all these, as to the gayer members of the group, the storm-tried veteran was sympathetic monitor and considerate friend."

*B*ut, fellow visitor from a later age, we must walk on. Our imaginary return to history is just at its beginning.

As one strolls the gentle slope, the lights of cottage rows dot the dark outline of adjoining hills. Listen and you hear music. Miss Mary Hagner (who wrote "The White Sulphur Papers" under the thoroughly un-belle-like penname of Mark Pencil, Esq.) tells of an evening party in the 1830's:

"The sound of Mr.—'s guitar in Paradise Row induced us to remain awhile to listen... 'Were it some hours later,' said B—, 'I should imagine the music proceeded from the lute of the White Phantom.' He was instantly called upon to explain. 'Do you not know,' replied he, 'that every dark night, as the clock strikes twelve, there is to be seen a phantom lady in white on the hill behind Paradise Row who walks slowly 'round the brow of it singing to a silver lute, sometimes a guitar? And should any serenader protract his song until that late hour, she immediately joins him in his hymn to beauty.'"

History does not tell us if this phantom joined her voice with that of Abram Van Buren, son of the president, on an early August evening in 1838. He and his friends are singing the traditional goodbye serenade to Miss Angelica Singleton, who is to leave White Sulphur the next day. And though the president himself is not singing in the serenade, he is listening from the colonnades of the Van Buren cottage next door. Let it be noted that Abram and Angelica had just become engaged.

In your imagination, walk on to the next cottage and move on forty years in time. It is 1878, and you see Governor Zebulon B. Vance of North Carolina visiting in the colonnaded cottage of Wade Hampton, governor of South Carolina. It is at White Sulphur Springs that the governor of North Carolina made his immortal comment. Today, we may honor it more in the breach than in the observance, for what he said to the governor of South Carolina may have been:

"It is now time to take a drink," instead of "It's a long time between drinks."

Walk on now, in this stroll through history, for the tour's next stop is across the central mall. It is time to witness invention of The Treadmill. No,

The Treadmill is not a source of power for a nearby grist mill—nor a hotel owner's way to extract his due. Let W. A. MacCorkle relate the tale:

"Legend says that Henry Clay offered his arm one night after supper to Mrs. John Preston, and that they marched around the big armchair that occupied the middle of the room. Mr. Calhoun then bowed over the hand of Mrs. Rhett of South Carolina and joined the procession. General John Preston invited Mrs. McFarlane of Richmond to walk a measure, and Mr. Randolph pressed Mrs. Chestnut of South Carolina to imitate their good friends. The beautiful Miss Caldwell...daughter of the Governor of Virginia, walked with [the future] Chief Justice Marshall, and after this leading, others fell in line...

"Henry Clay deemed The Treadmill a proper place to show courtesy to the wife of a doubtful supporter, and gave his arm to a country dame who blushed under her honors...and maybe whispering in his ear a recipe for souse, to which he listened with flattering attention."

In later years The Treadmill became social, "a place for the exhibition of beautiful toilettes, handsome figures and beautiful faces, a place where those who sat around and admired as, a few minutes before, they were admired when they took their turn, and saw all the great ones of the political or social or literary world."

*B*ut our evening walk through history goes on. On a rise of ground we see the Presidents' Cottage. There is President Tyler escorting his young bride Julia in the door. The couple's visit, soon after their marriage, is to give the cottage a name remembered far longer than the original Henderson House, for the rich Louisiana planter who built it.

And below this cottage, the center of it all, the white-pillared springhouse. What is more representative of White Sulphur than its spring? Though no longer the focus that everyone visits three times a day to drink the sulphur water, it remains the symbol of an era.

So think back, but only to 1948. It is April, and The Greenbrier—a hospital during most of World War II—has just reopened. Though it is late, you hear the click of many footsteps on the red brick walk. You see a group in formal clothes, led by a small, nimble man. Down the seven steps to the springhouse he goes, followed by his friends. He fills a glass from the spigot, and says:

"I first tasted this water when I visited White Sulphur in 1919 as Prince of Wales." He pauses, takes a drink from the glass, and makes a face. "It tastes just as bad now as it did then!" There is a ripple of laughter, a few join in tasting the water, and the group starts its merry trek back to The Greenbrier, the Duke of Windsor still in the lead.

In these days of antibiotic medicine, a former British monarch's memory of sulphur water may be a joking matter, but voices from a distant past demand their say.

Walk on some distance below the spring. It is 1778, and you see a woman crippled with rheumatism lying in a hollowed-out log. The family of this Mrs. Anderson, hearing that Indians believed these waters had miraculous curative powers, brought her here in a litter slung between two horses, for she was too ill to walk. Each day, her kin fill the tree trough with spring water and heat it for her with hot stones. The treatment works. Her condition improves, and swollen joints grow limber once again. When she leaves a few weeks hence, it will be astride her own horse.

MINERAL SPRINGS OF THE PAST

"...for what was
explorer Ponce de Leon's
fountain of youth
but a mineral spring?"

Though this 1778 rheumatic treatment marked the start of White Sulphur's modern fame, it is but a blink of an eyelid in the resort's total history. Nestled as it is in the Appalachian Mountains, White Sulphur Springs had its beginnings over a billion years ago.

It was a barren world of jagged black rocks, thrust up into immense mountain ranges by the slowly moving, viscous currents deep within the earth's molten core. As these currents pushed up the rocks and split them apart, the water within them was released, and when this vapor condensed, the first rains fell. Erosion started and rock sediments were borne down to the early seas, where they compacted and were raised once more.

Uplift and erosion. Uplift and erosion. As tens and hundreds of millions of years went by, great mountains were thrust up, and as the eons ticked on, these crags crumbled and again were washed away. Today's gentle Appalachian slopes are but the last remnants of mountains that were once miles high.

As the muddy mountain sediments cascaded down through the first land ferns, they formed a black layer of shale atop some sandstone, the ancient rock that brings us White Sulphur's waters.

Within these rocks, other changes were taking place. When water absorbed some carbon dioxide it became acidic, and thus was able to dissolve solid limestone rock. At times, large formations of limestone were eaten away, and underground caves were formed. There are fourteen such caverns known to exist in Greenbrier County, the largest

of them is Organ Cave, ten miles from White Sulphur. In this cave were discovered the bones of a prehistoric sloth—a beast which President Thomas Jefferson diffidently named the *Megalonyx Jeffersonii* in 1799.

But caves were the exceptions. More commonly, these acids would merely produce porous channels through which water could seep. It is through such porous paths that the mineral waters of White Sulphur Springs issue from the earth.

The mysterious manner in which waters from an unknown source will suddenly spring to the earth's surface was a subject for speculation—and superstitious worship—for centuries. To such early philosophers as Anaxagoras, Plato and Aristotle, spring waters issued from immense caverns within the earth. Later writers set "the virtue of the heavens" to work pulling water from the sea through hidden passages. This water then appeared as springs and rivers. It was only in the fifteenth and sixteenth centuries that such observers as Leonardo da Vinci and Bernard Palissy propounded the modern concept that while a great deal of rain water ran to the seas through streams and rivers, some of it seeped into the earth along the strata of sedimentary rocks, coming to the surface when unable to penetrate an impervious rock. Depending upon their underground course, some of these waters contained small amounts of dissolved minerals, others had considerable amounts.

The use of mineral waters is older than man himself, for the remains of arthritic dinosaurs have been found near the famous mineral springs of Tskhaltubo in the Caucasus. Perhaps it was instinct, or maybe some form of deductive reasoning that one animal communicated to the next. This chain extended to man when, long before the start

White Sulphur's famous springhouse may have been built as long ago as 1815, for a clipping found hidden within its columns tells about General Andrew Jackson's victory at New Orleans.

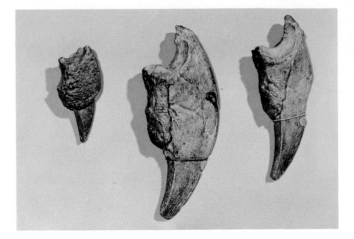

These teeth of a prehistoric sloth, discovered in a cave near White Sulphur Springs in 1799, are on display today at the Academy of Natural Sciences in Philadelphia.

of written history, someone chanced to observe that animals congregated near mineral springs as they did near salt licks.

Early historical documents in Egypt, Abyssinia, Persia, India and China mention treatment of disease by drinking and dunking. And these documents are quite specific as to which spring did best for what disease. Herodotus wrote that the springs of Tearos in Thrace cured skin complaints of men and animals; Pliny, that the Aenarian waters cured kidney stones and the waters of Thespiae, female sterility.

But if the Greeks were the first to systematize knowledge of the springs, the Romans were the ones who really utilized them. Wherever their empire spread, all sorts of bathing went along. In the East, Herod the Great tried to cure his illnesses in the Zerka Ma'in springs near the Dead Sea; in the West, Julius Caesar, during his campaign against the Gauls, enjoyed the waters of Vichy in France. Remains of Roman baths can also be found near springs in Spain, Switzerland and England; many of these spas would flourish long after the Roman Empire crumbled. The Spanish carried the tradition in a new direction, for what was explorer Ponce de Leon's fountain of youth but a mineral spring?

The English spring at Epsom became quite famous during the Restoration, and when Samuel Pepys visited it in July, 1663, he jotted down a comment typical of life at any popular spring: "But Lord! to see how many I met there of citizens that I could not have thought to have seen there, or that they had ever had it in their heads or purses to go down thither."

And with his statement that "We drank each of us two pots and so walked away, it being very pleasant to see how everybody turns up his tail," Pepys celebrated the action of mineral waters that when crystallized were to be called Epsom Salts.

*A*bout the time that Pepys was writing in his diary, settlers of New England were making pilgrimages to the first American spa—Stafford Springs, a town in northeast Connecticut that boasted two mineral waters. Further south, the Quakers had a wide choice. A 1698 geography of Pennsylvania tells of several springs, including one on what is now Willow Street in Philadelphia, "all out as good as Epsom." (The choice of phrase, one hopes, was unintentional.) But more famous among the Middle Atlantic springs of the early 1700's were those of Bristol and Yellow Springs, Pennsylvania, and the one on Schooley's Mountain, fifty miles across the river in New Jersey.

In 1748, an 18-year-old surveyor named George Washington visited the earliest of the Virginia springs—now Berkeley Springs. The notation in his diary indicates it was already popular, for he refers to it as "Ye Famed Warm Springs." This first Warm Springs soon changed its name to Frederick Springs, and in 1776 the state legislature changed it once again to Bath, in imitation of the English spa. In later years it became Berkeley Springs—and became part of West Virginia when the state was established in 1863. The Warm Spring Baths of today came along in 1761, and three years later, Sweet Springs, and in the next, Capon Springs. Soon there were many: Howard's Lick (once owned by Robert E. Lee's father), the Hot, the Healing, Salt Sulphur, Red Sulphur, Blue Sulphur and Gray Sulphur. But none was to capture the imagination of the public as did White Sulphur Springs in the years that followed 1778.

An attractive spring pavillion
is the keynote
of almost every health resort.
This old print shows
the redundantly named German
watering spot, Baden Baden.

The Romans disseminated their love
of mineral baths to all the
civilized world. These ancient
mineral pools were found
but a few feet below the modern
buildings of Bath, England.

Belgium's most famous mineral spring
has seen its name adopted as
the generic title
for all such establishments.
This is the bath house
in the resort city of Spa.

Bowyer &c
to } Deed
Bowyer &c

Examined

Whereas Michael Bowyer, deceased, late of the County of Greenbriar, departed this life, intestate, leaving the following Children to wit Jas Bowyer, Jno Bowyer, William Bowyer, Robert Bowyer, Mary Caldwell, wife of Jas Caldwell of the City of Baltimore; Fanny Beaford, wife of William Beaford, now of the County of Greenbriar and Elizabeth Copeland, widow of Jno Copeland deceased, late of the City of Baltimore, And Whereas the sd James Bowyer, upon a presumption that the legal Title to the real Estate of which his Father the said Michael died possessed, was in him did, convey to the sd Jno Bowyer & Mary his wife, Wm Beaford & Fanny his wife & Fanny his wife & Elizabeth Copeland, certain proportions of the Lands in the sd County of Greenbriar commonly called & known by the name of the Sulpher Spring Tract lying on Howards Creek a branch of Greenbriar River, which deed of Conveyance as appears in the County Court of Greenbriar a reference being thereto had, will more fully appear & whereas the sd Thomas Bowyer having taken the benefit of the act ...... for the relief of Insolvent debtors, in the sd County Court of Greenbriar, having .... did deliver in a Schedule of his Estate, both real and personal, which interest & term was sold, by the Sheriff of sd County by virtue of an order of said Court for the benefit of certain creditors of Thomas &c at which Sale, the sd William Beaford became the purchaser, and whereas doubts have arisen and disputes which are likely to arise among the above mentioned Heirs & representatives of the sd Michael Bowyer respecting the Title of the real Estate of which he died possessed being in manner quite uncertain, but no suit fully as settled any into the .... has arisen respecting the legal title to the real Estate of the said Michael Bowyer and the said Jas Bowyer, Jno Bowyer, Wm Bowyer, ... and Mary his wife, Wm Beaford, & Fanny his wife & Elizabeth Copeland have agreed that all the Lands & tenements of which the sd Michael Bowyer deceased died possessed, shall be equally divided between them having regard to quantity & quality by the Commissioners hereafter particularly chosen by them except the Tenements agreed to be laid off on the South side of Howards Creek of the aforesaid Sulpher Spring Tract which shall be laid off in convenient form so as to include the Sulpher Springs, the Houses, Barn & stables thereunto belonging & being as joint property together with part & parcel the body which two hundred acres with the appurtenances aforesaid, shall be held in common & for ever occupied, in such manner as a majority of the owners shall agree for the benefit of the whole. This Indenture therefore witnesseth, that the sd Jas Bowyer, & Fanny his wife, as Heirs in Common interest of the premises aforesaid, as of one, do each to them for have .... by each, the sd Jno Bowyer, William Bowyer, Jas Caldwell & Mary his wife, Wm Beaford, & Fanny his wife & Elizabeth Copeland the same of the said Jas Bowyer doth hereby acknowledge for party & considered

THE CAPTAIN'S DREAM

"White Sulphur... must be the largest
of the spring establishments
and, by all means,
the most important."

*I*t seems likely that the first non-Indians to explore the White Sulphur Springs vicinity were French from Canada, for the name Ronceverte appeared on Canadian maps some time before its equivalent, Greenbrier, was used on English ones. But whatever the language, the word referred to a brier that grows in tangled profusion in West Virginia. "Greenbrier, boldbrier, horsebrier, catbrier, squirrelbrier, devil's clothes line, whichever of its names you use," asserts White Sulphur naturalist Lyle Bryce, "it's a most troublesome bramble."

From the name of the brier came the name for the river, and for the mountain one sees from The Greenbrier's Golf and Tennis Club of today.

Though there were many who pushed through the Greenbrier vicinity along an old buffalo trail, the first large-scale attempt to settle the area was made at the urging of Virginia Governor Robert Dinwiddie. He helped a number of Augusta County residents set up the Greenbrier Land Company to obtain a grant of 100,000 acres on the Greenbrier River and its tributaries. In return, they were required to survey the area and settle a certain number of people on it. This type of grant was designed to provide men to fight to protect the border against Indians, for at the time, the frontier lay just a few miles west of Staunton. In addition, it was the governor's belief that such settlement would strengthen Virginia's claim to the lands east of the Ohio River, in opposition to the French claim on the Ohio-Mississippi Basin.

Some homesteaders anticipated this development. In 1750, when Dr. Thomas Walker visited

This Greenbrier County record of Michael Bowyer's death in 1809 is the first public document that mentions the presence of a mineral spring on the White Sulphur Springs property.

the area, he noted two things—bramble vines and settlers. From his journal for July 4:

"Greenbrier, We went up the River ten miles through very bad woods. 5th, The way being worse we traveled nine miles only. 6th, We left the river. The low grounds on it are of very little value, but on the Branches are very good in many places. We got to a large creek, which affords a great deal of very good land, and it is chiefly bought. We kept up the creek four miles and camped. There are some inhabitants on the Branches of the Green Bryer, but we missed their plantation."

Among those Walker missed was a Nicholas Carpenter, who, in 1749 or 1750, settled the White Sulphur Springs property on Howard's Creek, some five miles up from where it joins the Greenbrier River. He got it through what has been described as a "tomahawk title" or, more prosaically by "corn rights"—squatting on the land and farming it. Carpenter thought the spring was worthless. To him it was just a marshy spot that smelled of some strange decay. The important thing was the fertile bottomland. Moreover, the creek had enough of a drop to make a millrace and grist mill feasible. It was good land—even though there were too many big oak trees in the valley above that stinking spring to allow for easy cultivation.

While Carpenter was busy farming, the Greenbrier Land Company was also at work, and on April 10, 1751, it granted a 950-acre parcel that included the spring to a Samuel Howard. No controversy arose over Carpenter's farm at the time, for apparently he did not try to take possession before about 1755 when Fort Savannah was built eight miles away, near what later became the town of Lewisburg.

11

*Migrating buffalo laid out the Midland Trail,
which bisected the future lawn
of the White Sulphur Springs estate.
This drawing by the late Mrs. Perceval Reniers
telescopes a century of history—
from the age of Indian hunters
to the more sophisticated hoop-skirt era
at the region's watering places.
The trail later became U.S. Highway 60.*

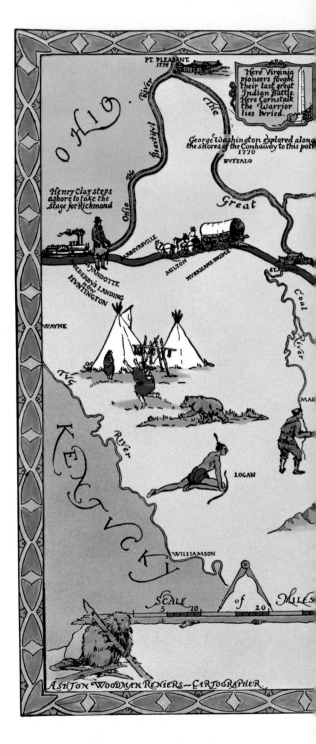

We know that Nicholas Carpenter had a wife named Kate who lived in Staunton, Virginia, during parts of her life, but there is no written record whether she ever accompanied her husband to the farm. If Nicholas allowed his wife and their one child to join him, he was foolhardy, or his wife uncommonly persuasive, for life on Howard's Creek was a risky business. Farms this far west of the frontier were continually subject to Indian raids and to depredation by white outlaws. But apparently she did come west with him.

What could have been expected to happen did happen. While Nicholas was away with the militia, marauding Indians attacked the valley. Kate, with her baby daughter Frances in her arms, fled to a nearby mountain. After several days in hiding, she left the slopes to find her way to a nearby settlement, later rejoining her husband. Nearby residents, in awe of so legendary an exploit, kept referring to the slope as Kate's Mountain, and the name, sometimes minus its apostrophe, is still used today.

Nicholas Carpenter died in the summer of 1752 while fighting Indians in a fort near Covington, Virginia. By some reports it was at this time that Kate, who was with him in the fort, escaped to her mountain; but with Covington some 25 miles east of Kate's Mountain, this version doesn't seem likely. History has been further muddled by the fact that there were two other, unrelated, Kate Carpenters in the area. One's husband was named Nathan; the second, William, whose family was killed or captured in a 1764 Indian raid.

In any case, *our* Kate Carpenter was back in Staunton in the mid-fifties, for it was there she raised her Frances into the beautiful young woman who married Michael Bowyer in 1766.

Young Bowyer owned a general store in Fincastle, Virginia, but to refer to him merely as a storekeeper does him an injustice. He was also a farmer, lawyer, officer in the Augusta County militia, and church vestryman. In 1773, he was elected to the county governing board, and, after

12

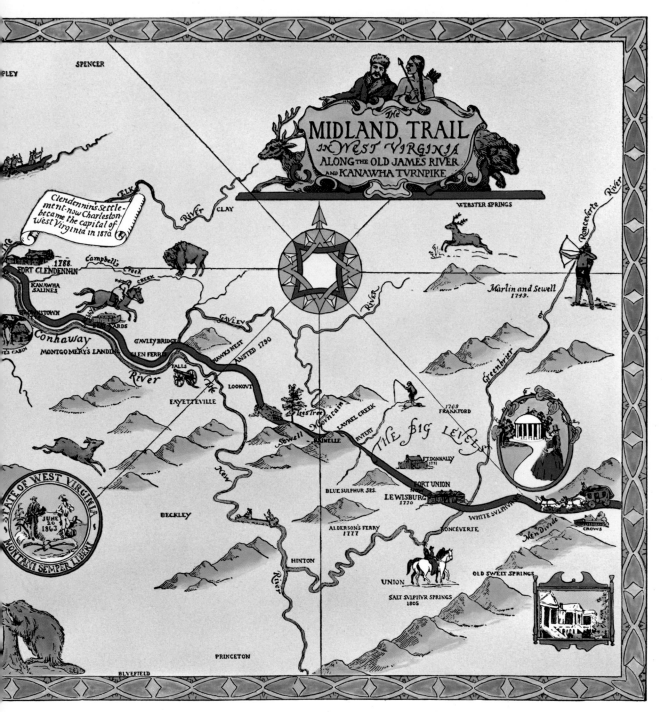

Drawing by Ashton Woodman Reniers for "The Midland Trail," © 1926, 1954. Reproduced by permission.

the Revolutionary War, to the state legislature. During the war, he served as a captain.

At the time Bowyer returned home from the war in 1781, he knew nothing about Mrs. Anderson's miraculous cure at White Sulphur Springs three years before. But after discussing plans with his wife, they decided to move west and farm the White Sulphur acreage. They persuaded her mother to sell him the property, and she did so on March 22, 1782. When he rode out to look over his purchase, he found others on the land who, as the assignees of the Greenbrier Land Company, dis-

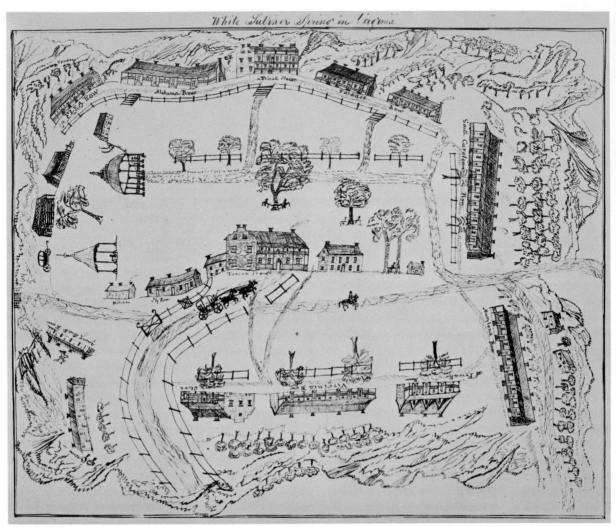

This primitive map represents White Sulphur in the 1820–1830 period. Note the two springhouses at upper left, with the Alabama Row Cottages immediately above, and the private house (now the Presidents' Cottage Museum) and Paradise Row to the right.

puted his claim. They went to court, and Bowyer won. On May 22, 1783, the Virginia Court of Appeals in Richmond confirmed his claim, and he obtained patent to the 950 acres on February 21, 1784.

But while Bowyer was making ready to move his family to White Sulphur, tragedy struck. Both Frances and Mother Kate died within a year. This set back his plans, and it was not until several years later that he finally moved west. In the meantime, reports continued to reach him about the number of people who were visiting the spring and building log or brush shelters on his property. Thus, though he had clear title to the land, he hired a Mr. and Mrs. Gibson to occupy it as his agents. It was their son who wrote what may be the earliest description of life at White Sulphur Springs:

The Spring, then in its natural state, emptied its water from between two flag rocks about twenty inches wide and about four inches apart, falling into a pool about three feet deep. Thus it remained for years after without any artificial alteration. I never saw the spring muddy—the changes of the weather had no effect in increasing or diminishing the quantity of water.

"At the time my father moved to the White the only improvements on the property were a few small log cabins—the principal one of which was to be occupied by our family. Most of those who came to the Springs brought tents, provisions and cooking utensils on pack horses—no arrangements being yet made to board visitors. From twenty to thirty persons came during the warm season. My parents remained there three years... After my father's departure, Mr. Bowyer moved his family and occupied the Springs property."

Bowyer and his brood of ten children arrived in 1788, bringing with them two friends, a Mr. and Mrs. Wiley. That year two cabins and a stable were built on the property—Bowyer putting up a single cabin for his family; Wiley building a double cabin, half for rental. It thus appears that Wiley was the first man to recognize that money could be made by catering to invalids and travelers. And both were coming along the nearby Midland Trail in ever-increasing numbers.

In the beginning, this trail was a varmint path, used by animals in their migrations or in expeditions to nearby valleys for food and mineral licks; even the animals, it appears, had some difficulty in penetrating the greenbrier vines. As the larger animals trod the paths along which their smaller brothers had scurried, the trail became better marked. Soon the Indians found it, and long before the white man came, there was a well-traveled mountain path connecting the James River Basin of eastern Virginia with the Kanawha and Ohio Valleys further west. This was the route that was followed, in the most part, by Andrew Lewis when he blazed the trail in 1754. By 1782, a road had been added—a "road" in the kind sense of the word, for just about all that had been done was to chop down some small trees. The road detoured around the larger trees and rocks, and during rainy seasons it was impassable. The road received little maintenance and, as the years went on, became worse and worse. So the state intervened. Stumps were removed and some levelling carried out. And with the opening in 1790 of what became known as the State Road, travel increased substantially—as it was to do again when the James River and Kanawha Turnpike opened over the same route in 1824. Lyle Bryce's picture is a colorful one:

"There were landgrabbers, speculators, trappers, traders, people one jump ahead of the sheriff, gamblers, fancy women, corn doctors, jugglers, magicians, small circuses, museums, army officers headed to western posts. Twenty-four hours a day, seven days a week, the whole road was really a carnival, a circus. But it mirrored the history of a nation during its early expansive years."

Small wonder, that with such a procession moving only a few hundred feet away from the spring, there were increasing requests for lodging. Wiley could always rent out the extra half of his cabin, and soon found the demand so great that he rented all of it and moved into the stable. More people came, and finding no place to stay, pleaded with Wiley through the cracks in the stable walls for the privilege of sleeping in the hay.

As traffic on the trail and early road continued to expand, Wiley persuaded Bowyer to build more cabins to meet the demand from transients as well as from those who came to drink or bathe.

It was all quite rustic and wild. Often a deer or two were shot from the edge of the clearing before breakfast, and it was common to see wolves and panthers prowling around the cabins in broad daylight. One of the latter got so bold that it chased Mrs. Wiley into a cabin.

There was a marsh below the spring, and once Wiley's horse was swamped in mud so deep that only its head and ears were visible. Needless to say, as soon as he freed the horse, Wiley cleaned out the spring. It is probable that he discovered a second, milky-white spring at this time, for there are two sulphur springs on the property within a hundred feet of each other. The white spring gave its name to the resort, but the clear-watered one was the original spring—the one we know today.

There is no record that either Bowyer or Wiley ever took out a license to operate a tavern. Nonetheless, quite an establishment was growing up, for when Bowyer's estate was appraised after his death in 1809, it included, among other items:

7 large dining tables
25 small tables
48 candlesticks
64 dinner plates
29 butter plates
21 soup bowls
48 knives and forks
11 wash bowls
38 cots
23 mattresses
674 lbs. of pillows and bolsters
48 blankets
45 counterpanes
70 sheets
and 1 chamber pot.

This 1832 watercolor by Architect John H. B. Latrobe accurately depicts White Sulphur's original tavern. The roadway that runs in front of it now leads from The Greenbrier down to the Golf and Tennis Club.

One day in the early 1790's, three citified young men rode up to Michael Bowyer's log-cabin establishment. William Bedford, James Calwell, and John Copeland were out scouting the rapidly developing nation west of the Alleghenies, for things had not gone too well for them further east. Bedford and Calwell had chartered some sailing vessels to trade between Baltimore and the East Indies, but they had gone broke. So with Copeland, who had been their chief clerk, they were looking for new trading opportunities. "And how little," wrote a later historian, "did Mr. Bowyer realize the bright future in store for his three rosy-cheeked, barefoot daughters that huddled behind the door when these shipping merchants were taking their first meal in his cabin." The future that the barefoot Fanny, Polly and Betsy Bowyer had in mind was wedlock, for they married all three. Calwell, after his marriage to Polly in 1797, took his bride back to Baltimore, where, for the moment, he leaves our tale.

The next few years were busy ones at White Sulphur, for Bowyer was building more cabins for his ever-increasing trade. Some time after June, 1808, he completed his main tavern building. (Parts of this building still stand; they are incorporated

into the Lester Building, used as an employee residence.)

Bowyer died that winter. Ann Royall, a travelling writer, tells the sad story: "Old Mr. Bowyer... died sitting upright in his chair. How long before it was discovered no one knew as he was alone."

The White Sulphur property was taken over by his son, James. But he immediately divided it up with the three of his sisters who had married the boys from Baltimore. Each sister paid him the nominal sum of a dollar for 200-acre plots of fertile bottomland in the sections of the estate that today are The Greenbrier's golf courses. A 16-acre plot that included the spring and the grist mill was set aside for joint use with his three sisters and their families.

The transfer of Bowyer property to the Baltimore wing of the family gave sea trader James Calwell a voice in management. At his urging, a Mr. Harrington of eastern Virginia was given a five-year lease to the spring. One condition of Harrington's lease was that he erect ten new cottages, each 18 by 20 feet, with brick chimney and shingled roof. They were begun in the winter of 1810, and were ready for guests by July 20. During that 1811 season we have an early note of the

This Latrobe rendering shows both of the early springhouses (center). The tavern is off to the left, stables can be seen in the center behind the springs and an edge of the Paradise Cottage Row is shown at far right.

spring's popularity. People were already being sent out to board at nearby farmhouses.

By the time Harrington's lease expired in 1815, Calwell was trying to buy out the other three heirs. Perhaps he had made money during the 1812–1815 war, but if his later fund-raising efforts were part of a pattern, he borrowed it. Calwell soon moved back to White Sulphur with his wife and eleven children (a twelfth was to be born there). Having obtained a $20,000 loan in 1817—eight Baltimore friends co-signed the notes—he ordered that the tavern be expanded and a springhouse built.

White Sulphur's first springhouse was a wooden affair built over the milky spring. It was a square, four-pillared structure with a pyramid-like roof. On the pinnacle resided a life-size carving of an Indian queen in full regalia. In her right hand she held a bundle of arrows and in her left, a large bowl. This unpainted spring house was to last only into the early 1800's. By then, the domed structure we know today had been erected over the other spring. Atop it was placed a statue of Hygeia, goddess of health.

Though the year in which this springhouse was built is not known, it seems to bear some relationship to the career of a noted White Sulphur visitor,

President Andrew Jackson. A sealed box that contained clippings about General Jackson's part in the Battle of New Orleans was found within a springhouse pillar during its reconstruction in 1964. One of Jackson's visits to southwestern Virginia occurred in October, 1815, only a few months after the battle.

Another of White Sulphur's favorite v.i.p.'s visited the property on July 20, 1817, soon after Calwell had begun to interest himself in its operation. Henry Clay, then speaker of the House of Representatives, arrived enroute from Washington to his home in Kentucky. Like Robert E. Lee fifty years later and like the Duke of Windsor in modern times, Clay was one of the spring's pivotal guests— a "tastemaker" whose imprimatur brought many others to White Sulphur.

That year, Clay arrived with a servant and three horses for a visit that lasted three days. The ledger entry of this visit is worth recounting in detail for the picture it gives of those times. Clay's room and board cost $1.50 a night (a total of $4.50). Lodging his servant and stabling the three horses cost 75¢ each per night ($9). The horses ate two gallons of grain on the day of departure (33¢), and nine

Henry Clay was a favorite guest at the spring. His 1817 stopover was noted in one early ledger that still exists.

Henry Clay Servant &
3 Horses arrived to Breakfast
1817 20th July
July 20th Dram per Servant 12½
         1 Dozen Segars   25
   20   Commenced 3 Extra gallons grain
   23rd Do for Washing   68½
         2 Grogs per Servant   12½

         3 Days Board @ $1.50 — 4.50
         Same for Servant @ 75 — 2.25
         Same time for 3 Horses
         @ 75 Cts Each p day   6.75
         1 Gall Extra Grain —   1.50
                               $16.18½
                                    33
   23   By Cash in full $16.51½
                               $16.51½

more gallons of feed were taken along ($1.50). Clay bought a dozen cigars (25¢) and had his clothes laundered (68½¢). His servant had three drinks, a dram of brandy upon arrival (12½¢) and two grogs (6¼¢ each). The grand total for three days was $16.51½.

One question this account raises is whether Clay himself was abstaining. It is far more likely he was drinking with his friend James Calwell.

It was said that guests did not honor Calwell by coming to visit his White Sulphur Springs, but that he honored them by allowing them to come. Henry Clay was one of the few favorite guests whom he would invite out of altruism to visit his quarters for a glass of wine or, perhaps, a hailstorm —that early-day White Sulphur version of the mint julep. Most of the others Calwell so honored were men from whom he wanted a loan.

Contemporaries describe Calwell as a ruddy-faced, dumpy little man, placid in disposition, old-fashioned in appearance. Until his death in 1851 he appeared in knee britches and wore his hair in a queue, tied back with a narrow black ribbon—a coiffure more suited to a colonial gentleman of 1773 than to a baby born in that year.

Calwell was a dreamer, not a businessman. He was not a much better hotel proprietor than he was a sea trader, a profession at which he went broke. But he dreamed big dreams about White Sulphur. It must be the largest of the spring establishments and, by all means, the most important.

When one looks back at the pluses and minuses of Calwell's reign at the White Sulphur Springs, six reasons for success are apparent: the spring, the road, money, nabobs, the climate, and the belles.

The spring itself came first, for unlike some other Virginia springs, it had a noticeable sulphur odor—"like a half-boiled, half-spoiled egg." One of the legends has it that a southern Bobby Shaftoe who walked near the spring for a time found that his silver buckles had tarnished. And soon after this report came a more wondrous one. People who had been drinking the White Sulphur water found that silver coins *in their pockets* had turned black.

The second reason was the road. Though there had been a constant stream of visitors ever since the early trail and the state road had been open, it took the construction of the James River and Kanawha Turnpike in 1824 to really set things going. In 1816, almost all the travelers were men—usually two men riding together or a man with his servant. There were some parties with women and a few with children, but judging from the number of horses that accompanied each of these groups, it is obvious they were not there just for vacation. They were traveling by wagon, on their way to

This likeness of James Calwell was made some months before his death in 1851.

Calwell, like many of his relatives, is buried in the cemetery atop White Sulphur's Copeland Hill.

settle in what was then still western Virginia, or in Kentucky, Ohio, Indiana and points beyond. But with the turnpike, things changed. One could travel by scheduled stage coach or with one's own carriage. Now, whole families travelling together could use the new road to the springs. Henry Clay provides a good example. Though he arrived at White Sulphur in 1817 with a servant and one extra horse, he was to make his 1832 entry with wife, grandson, four servants, two carriages, six horses, a shepherd dog and a jackass.

The third reason for Calwell's success was his customers' prosperity. During most of the twenties and thirties, the prices paid for the South's crops were rising to unheard-of heights.

In the fourth place, there were nabobs. Though money was important in making a nabob, it was not all; one had to be an aristocrat. Henry Clay was certainly nabob-in-chief, but the fact that he usually didn't stay at White Sulphur for an entire summer season put others in the race. One who qualified was Colonel Richard Singleton of South Carolina. By 1825, Calwell had built the Singletons a private, two-story cottage with Grecian colonnades out front, and the family began its 28-year taste-making reign at The White. All of this pleased the proprietor, for Singleton was an easy touch.

Fifth, were the tidewater epidemics. Cholera swept the nation in 1832, making its start along Hampton Roads, then moving on up Chesapeake Bay and the rivers to Richmond, Washington and Baltimore. Yellow fever raged in New Orleans, followed by cholera. But as the cities and plantations tried to cope with these outbreaks, the word got around that, for some unknown reason, the Virginia springs were free from pestilence. Reasons

be damned! Off to the springs! And those who visited these watering places for the first time found that the scenery and the sociability were to their liking. Some even enjoyed the spring water. And so a habit was begun.

Sixth and finally, the southerner is a gregarious person, and the life, at least on plantations, gave few opportunities to mix with others of one's class. So visits to the springs gave parents a chance to arrange a suitable marriage for their daughters.

For these reasons, guests flocked to the White Sulphur Springs—something that should have made James Calwell famous, happy and rich. Fame he got, happiness maybe, but riches were always to elude him. Alas, he never even got free of that $20,000 borrowed back in 1817. By his death in 1851, Calwell had pyramided his debts to $400,000, a substantial sum by today's standards, but a staggering one for his era.

The start of Calwell's problems was generally out of his control, for in prosperous 1817 who but the blackest pessimist could have anticipated the 1819 panic, and a depression so bad that three out of four factory workers would be unemployed. But more of the problem was that he was no manager. In his haste to expand, he forgot to keep enough cash on hand. A further drain on his money was his family, for they, like the offspring of Michael Bowyer one generation back, had a taste for high living. When his son John won $500 on a lottery ticket, he bought 50 custom-tailored vests.

As Lewis Carroll's Red Queen remarked: "It takes all the running you can do to keep in the same place." And James Calwell was not much of a runner. Goodness knows he tried, but his only answer was to build more cottages. "It appears I cannot do too much in this way," he wrote to his

creditor Singleton, "as the company always over-runs the room. I shall continue the improvements although I am not yet clear of my difficulties."

With so much effort going into construction of new buildings, Calwell let his control of other parts of the operation slip. A modern administrator might have decided to consolidate, improving services and raising prices commensurately, but none of this occurred to Calwell. Thus, in a year when Calwell had money in his pocket, service improved; when he was feeling the usual pinch, things were not too good for most guests.

The southern nabobs couldn't have cared less. They had private cottages that Calwell built for them at a cost of $100 or so, and these were their own whenever they arrived. The nabobs paid the normal charge for room and board, even if they had foresightedly brought along their own cook. But for others it could be grim.

Perhaps the worst review that the Calwell days received came from the man who founded the future New York Central Railroad, George W. Featherstonhaugh. If not the worst, it was certainly the longest, for he devoted thirty-five pages of one of his books to this denunciation. Featherstonhaugh thought he had a place reserved, since a mutual friend had written the proprietor to introduce him. But he found differently upon arrival, when Calwell's major-domo, "the Metternich of the mountains," turned him down flat: "Look ye, Mister, I han't room for a cat, to say nothing about your family."

This panorama of White Sulphur Springs
as seen from atop Copeland Hill
was painted by Edward Beyer
in about 1850. It is a forerunner
of the engraving in his "Album of Virginia,"
a famous portfolio of ante-bellum
southern scenes.
The painting now hangs in The Greenbrier's
Presidents' Cottage Museum.

around us"), the evening dancing ("young persons who love to dance can amuse themselves very well: for the musicians are far above the Ordinary"), and the meals served in a nearby shanty by a former Baltimore oyster cook named Wright: "I have... had the justest cause to admire his skill in venison steaks, mutton chops and in the concoction of inimitable ice punch... indeed all the appliances of a jolly existence... At the period of my departure, Mr. Wright was becoming a formidable rival to the bar-room of the White Sulphur."

Other British travellers of the 1830's were far more kind. Miss Harriet Martineau, in her "Society in America," wrote that everybody "was gay and spruce... the gentlemen in the piazza in glossy coats and polished pumps; ladies in pink, blue and white, standing on green grass, shading their delicate faces and gay head-dresses under parasols...

"There was less meat on the table at breakfast and tea than I was accustomed to see. The bread and tea were good. For the other eatables there is little to be said. It is a table spread in the wilderness; and a provision of tender meat and juicy vegetables for two or three hundred people is not to be had for the wishing. The dietary is sure to be improved from year to year."

𝒫erhaps this controversy between Britons can best be summed up by Mark Pencil:

"Foreigners, travelling, generally have very singular notions about us... whoever goes forth in search of the curious and the picturesque will be most certain to find it."

Shunted for five days to the nearby home of a surly blacksmith, Featherstonhaugh climaxed his daily visits to Metternich with a threat that "if I was not taken in forthwith, I should leave the White Sulphur altogether; but desired him to understand that it was my fixed purpose to leave such a memorandum upon his shoulders as would be talked of by all who visited the mountains for generations to come." It is almost a pity that Featherstonhaugh eventually got in, for his memorandum could hardly have been worse. His description of Calwell's tavern, for example, was that of a "miserable looking sort of barrack, badly constructed of wood, with a dilapidated portico".

About the only good things Featherstonhaugh had to report were the scenery ("sweet views

21

NABOBS, PEERS AND PRESIDENTS

"When, lo, who should unexpectedly arrive
but Henry Clay—the bold and
dauntless Clay, who took pride in outfacing
his enemies..."

If it was White Sulphur's sylvan setting that brought the people each summer, it was the people who made White Sulphur. For the right ones were there. Some were from the North, from the rapidly settling Midwest, or from Europe, but most of all, they were from the South.

"Southern aristocrats came out in all their splendor to pass the summers, like grand old Southern gentlemen all of the olden time," an early chronicler wrote. "They came from eastern Virginia and the tobacco plantations, and from the rice and cotton plantations of South Carolina and Georgia [not to mention the sugar plantations of Louisiana]. There was the coachman and the ladies' maid, and sometimes the family cook, and a merry, dignified, proper time they had of it then. No schottische, no German, no round dancing, but the decent Old Virginia reel. No strychnine, no adulterations, but the genuine home-distilled apple brandy, or pure port and madeira of one's own im-

---

Eight presidents are reckoned among the famous visitors to White Sulphur in the years before the Civil War. The guests shown in the photograph at left are (1) Miss Betsy Patterson, sister-in-law to Napoleon, (2) Daniel Webster, (3) Millard Fillmore, (4) Andrew Jackson, (5) James Buchanan, (6)

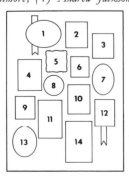

Thomas Hart Benton, (7) Miss Angelica Singleton, who became daughter-in-law of (8) Martin Van Buren, (9) Miss Julia Gardiner, second wife of (10) John Tyler, (11) Zachary Taylor, (12) Franklin Pierce, (13) James K. Polk, and (14) last, but certainly not the least, Henry Clay.

portation. And so they came to Greenbrier and spent their money freely, and bought the fine Greenbrier horses to put to their carriages, and on the first day of September back they went to their places, to come again the next year."

One of the early nabobs, Colonel William Pope of Alabama, contributed to White Sulphur's legends by inventing the Billing, Wooing and Cooing Society. He set up a list of respectable gentlemen to whom a young man had to be known to be listed as a society member. Soon after the society's constitution had been inscribed on a special scroll of pink paper and hung on the ballroom wall, it had appended a list of 1,700 eligible young men. And though dancing was never on Sunday, the scroll kept its place on the wall during the sabbath service. "It was said to be as salutary as any sermon," Perceval Reniers relates in *The Springs of Virginia*, "reminding young men whose eyes wandered to the wall that in that Constitution were set down the rules that must govern a gentleman pursuing a lady. For transgressors it was a silent, pink rebuke; no preacher was so eloquent."

Pope also directed the dances, setting up cotillion figures so intriguing that most everyone forgot or ignored round dances like the waltz. Late in the season, when interest in dancing often flagged, Pope would march the band round the green, gathering up the young like the Pied Piper of old.

At times White Sulphur was more than social. The up-and-coming young lawyers were there, making the acquaintance of men of substance who would be able to help their careers.

And in the summer of 1837, during the panic that followed the controversy over whether to recharter the Bank of the United States, President Van Buren and his advisors met at White Sulphur.

*The Presidents' Cottage—so named
to honor its famous early residents—
is today The Greenbrier's museum.
Some rooms are furnished with authentic
period furniture; others contain
murals and photographic print displays.*

Out of their discussion evolved the modern monetary system and the U.S. Treasury of today.

White Sulphur's people best characterize those early years. Much of what we know about them comes from newspaper reports, contemporary books and from personal letters in various libraries and collections. To these well-known items can now be added a source which has never before been made public—a memoir by the physician at White Sulphur for over 40 years, Professor John J. Moorman, M. D. Moorman is best known for his book on mineral springs that went through seven editions and numerous printings in the years between 1839 and 1873.

One of Moorman's close friends was James Barbour, a governor of Virginia whose oratorical eloquence gained him fame as The Thunderer. While Barbour was journeying to the springs by stagecoach, he described to a fellow passenger, "an intellectual and fashionable Northern lady," the qualities of the springs—the White, the Red, the Blue, the Warm, the Hot, the Sweet and the Salt.

"I then observed," said he, "there is another spring in the County of Rockingham called 'Rawley Spring' that has a good deal of reputation."

She said, "Pray, Governor, what are the qualities of the Rawley water?"

"Well, Madam," he replied, "I can only say of the Rawley Spring, that if it had been known in the days of our Old Father Abraham, there would have been no occasion for a Special Revelation to Sarah."

Moorman wrote of two speeches made in Richmond to promote the presidential candidacy of William Henry "Tippecanoe" Harrison, one by Barbour, the second by another White Sulphur visitor, Daniel Webster. During Barbour's oration,

Professor John J. Moorman, M.D., who spent 40 summers supervising mineral water treatments at White Sulphur, wrote a never-before-published memoir on famous visitors to the springs.

"I saw all around me persons weeping as though they had just heard of some deeply sorrowful event or of news so gladdening that it forced the tears with a smile." Webster's speech, though far more substantial than Barbour's, caused no one to weep.

It was during Webster's visit to Virginia that he went to "a wine frolic" and questioned his host, General Drumgold, on what made one well liked in the state: "I am told, General, that I am not popular in Virginia, and I cannot well account for it, for I am sure I am very Virginian in all my tastes and habits—I drink, I fail to pay my debts, and I am not over scrupulous of my marital relations. Such qualities, I would think, ought to make me very popular with Virginians."

But it is in recollections of presidents who visited White Sulphur that Moorman's memoir is especially interesting:

"President Pierce spent some time at the Springs. He was what you might call a nice little gentleman, always nice and tidy in his dress and nice in his manners. I think nice rather than elegant is the word for his manners. He made himself very agreeable to his associates, and was always kindly and attentive to all around him. He was a sprightly man with some cleverness without being great, I think, in any department of mind.

"Mr. Fillmore, who spent some time at the Springs during his presidency, was a lusty, farmer-like man of good manners and genial temper. He was a gentleman of fine sense and of fair cultivation—a conservative and safe man in public position; not particularly brilliant in intellect, but never falling below great respectability."

The man whom Fillmore succeeded in the presidency, Zachary Taylor, was not only a visitor to White Sulphur, but a recommender of it. Once when his brother Hancock Taylor and family were visiting springs in Kentucky, he wrote that if those springs "have not the effect of re-establishing yours and their health, that you will extend your visit to White Sulphur Springs in Virginia."

Moorman, who, in the company of Governor Wood and Senator Sam Houston, visited Taylor in the White House, felt that he had spent too much of his life in the backwoods:

I have rarely seen anyone that looked less prepossessing or less at ease. After the introduction, there was nothing said by anyone for some time, when Governor Wood, evidently to break the monotony, said, 'Mr. President, I lately saw Major Hays at Matamoras.' 'Oh,' said the president, 'what is he driving at there?' Governor Wood told what Major Hays was 'driving at,' and the conversation flagged. Presently the governor tried again, 'I met your old friend Colonel Soandso in Nashville not long ago and he is married.' 'Ah,' said the president, slightly raising his head, 'who did he pick up?' Wood told him whom he had 'picked up,' and the conversation again flagged. Houston and myself walked out on the back porch, and he jocularly expatiated for a moment how he would lord it over the White House if he were president of the United States."

But if Taylor was uncommunicative, Van Buren was noncommittal. Though Moorman "was much in his company" for the six weeks in 1837 that the president was at White Sulphur, "he was entirely unaggressive in manner and language, and reticent to a degree beyond any other public man I have known. I do not remember ever to have heard Mr. Van Buren express a bold or even decided opinion in reference to any measure or man."

Van Buren, his Cabinet, and many congressmen were guests of honor at a "pic-nic" for nearly a hundred persons. As Mark Pencil recorded it:

"The party had all assembled before two o'clock at the brick tavern at the bridge [where the James River and Kanawha Turnpike crossed the Greenbrier River]. Parties on pic-nic excursions generally carry their own delicacies and baskets, but this was to be an uncommon affair. We found everything amply provided for us, as it were by invisible hands. Invisible hands had got ready the most tempting and cooling beverages for the dusty, thirsty guests (it was a very dusty day), and invisible hands had prepared, under a large green arbor at the foot of the mountain, a most magnificent entertainment. And then with myrtle leaves for a canopy over our devoted heads, we all sat down with smiling faces to do justice to the delicacies spread before us. We had all the luxuries of the mountains, the farm-yard, and the streams."

But the spell was slightly broken. The invisible hands belonged to noisy servants, who had to "duel with the corks to the champagne." The table, however, "was sparkling with wine and wit."

John Tyler's second wife, Julia—thirty years her husband's junior but still destined to bear him seven children—chafed under the "whiggish atmosphere" of White Sulphur. She felt she had to "be dignified as an Ex-Queen and sit with the Old Ladies, when I was dying to join in the mirth of the younger ones... I went... dressed in black, and have not attended again."

Moorman reported that Tyler, on one of his visits, "was located to his satisfaction on the grounds, and for a few days seemed to be enjoying himself greatly, he was literally the lion of the grounds. When, lo, who should unexpectedly arrive but Henry Clay—the bold and dauntless Clay, who took pride in outfacing his enemies and who was well-known as the political and even personal enemy of Mr. Tyler."

There is some disagreement on what happened next. Moorman says that "all attention was at once turned" to Clay, but one of the Tyler party wrote that "Clay was not received as enthusiastically as one would have thought, and I fear greatly that he will never be President—so git-long, Clay."

Tyler, however, seemed to have agreed more with Moorman, who wrote: "Mr. Tyler, evidently

chagrined, stood this for a few days, but only for a few, and then having his baggage loaded upon a stagecoach at the very instant that a large crowd with a band of music was surrounding Mr. Clay's cottage, drove—unattended, and as silent as a funeral procession—through the grounds to reach the highway of exit from the Springs." So git-long, Tyler.

Clay, of all White Sulphur guests, seems to have struck the most responsive chord in Moorman, for there is a particular warmth of description:

"Mr. Clay, when first I knew him, had rather passed in age what we term 'middle life'—but was still in the prime of noble manhood, and in the full vigor of his intellectual powers. He was tall of stature, full six feet, I think, in height; spare and erect; remarkable for a somewhat prominent nose, thin lips and an uncommonly large mouth. To his contemporaries, I need not speak of this latter feature, for everyone knew very well that his mouth was fully capable of speaking for itself...

"On one occasion, an elegant lady, the wife of Captain Wood of the army, and a great admirer of Mr. Clay, was very desirous of getting a lock of his hair... I delivered her note.

"The next day, meeting Mrs. Wood, it was delightful to see the old gentleman (for his locks were then quite gray) exhibiting all the gallantry of a young man of twenty in delivering the lock to Mrs. Wood. Upon her offering to apologize for the trouble she had given him, with one of his blandish smiles, he said, 'Oh, Madam, don't mention it—it has been a very great pleasure to me—and I beg you to believe that not only a lock of my hair, but my heart, and all I am are yours, except only my hand which is Mrs. Clay's.'"

Clay's gallantry here reminded Moorman of his response to a fulsome compliment paid him by a newly-introduced lady: "Why, madam, said he, you quite confound me by your flattering estimate of myself—and remind me that one of my good friends in Washington, Lord Morpeth, is almost as remarkable as myself for having a very ugly mouth. Two of my lady friends were talking one day about him. One said to the other, 'Now, Jane, what would you take to kiss that ugly mouth of Lord Morpeth's?' 'Why, Annie, I would not do it for the whole world.' 'Now would you do it to make Mr. Clay president of the United States?' 'Yes, Annie, to do that, *I'd go it*.'"

Lord Morpeth was the first of British royalty and aristocracy to be intrigued with life at White Sulphur Springs. As a result, he stretched his 1842 visit to six weeks. Baron Renfrew, the name used by King Edward VII during his 1860 visit to the United States, is said to appear on White Sulphur's rolls, though we know more about the visits of his grandson, King Edward VIII. Lord Morpeth, the seventh Earl of Carlisle, celebrated his sojourn with these "brief Farewell lines to the small temple-like cupola over the bright sulphur well:

"Hail dome! whose unpresuming circle guards
Virginia's flowing fountain: still may health
Hover above thy crystal urn, and bring
To cheeks unused their bloom! may Beauty still
Sit on thy billowy swell of wooded hills,
And deep ravines of verdure; may the axe,
Improvement's necessary pioneer,
Mid forest solitudes, still gently pierce,
Not bare their leafy bowers! This votive lay
Like wreath of old on thy white columns hung.
Albeit of scentless flowers from foreign soil,
Scorn not, and bid the Pilgrim pass in peace."

BAPTISM BY FIRE

"...the seasons at White Sulphur
became more brilliant—
perhaps in unconscious apprehension of
the dreary war years ahead."

*B*y 1850 it was obvious that a real hotel would have to be built at White Sulphur Springs, for though business had lagged during the depressed forties, it was again above capacity. James Calwell saw the construction of a big hotel as his only salvation. So the plans were drawn, and the 77-year-old Calwell once again began inviting friends in for a glass of wine and a sales talk amid the blueprints. We shall never know whether he could have raised this new money for he died in 1851, his goal unreached. William Calwell, his son and general manager, tried to carry on, but all he got for his efforts were threats of foreclosure.

The creditors, moreover, wouldn't even let things go on as they had, so Calwell finally hit on the plan of a public stock sale. In 1853, he got the legislature in Richmond to pass an act setting up The White Sulphur Springs Company and authorizing sale of $500,000 worth of stock, but it soon became apparent that this would not be enough to pay all his debts and build a new hotel besides. So back to Richmond. In 1854, the legislature passed a more liberal act of incorporation—one that allowed sale of three times as much stock.

With this in hand, negotiations began in earnest. First it was a Yankee syndicate that was interested, but nothing happened. Then some men from Baltimore, but nothing happened. Next some of those perennially-fascinated Britishers came in for a look, but nothing happened. By 1856, the property was being advertised for sale in the newspapers. Finally, on May 1, 1857, came the sale. Not to northerners, Baltimore businessmen, foreigners, but to

eight fellow Virginians, including the famed Commodore Matthew Fontaine Maury. The price was $200,000 in cash, which went to James Calwell's heirs and to Frances Bedford and Elizabeth Copeland, daughters of Captain Michael Bowyer—for it appears that Calwell never acquired their interests. The creditors—whose insistence on cash had blocked all previous attempts at sale—ended up with $400,000 in new promissory notes.

The eight new owners also put up $120,000 in cash, and in 1857, they broke ground for a magnificent new hotel.

It was advertised as the largest building in the South; the largest hotel in all the United States. The parlor was half again as large as the "celebrated East Room" of the White House. Legend had it that the dining room was so immense that waiters were forced to serve on horseback. This "stupendous building" was The Old White.

Unfortunately for the sake of legend, that was not its name. For the spring's new proprietors were fascinated by two words that expressed the hopes of hotel owners everywhere. So it was the Grand Central Hotel that opened in June of 1858.

But just as was to happen to the Grand Central Hotel in Bar Harbor, no one paid any attention. In Maine, the hotel was called Rodick's after its builder. In Virginia, it became The White, after its spring.

Nothing daunted White Sulphur's owners. Though there was a time around 1880 when their brochures merely advertised the White Sulphur Springs Hotel, even as late as 1887 the stationery supplied to guests adamantly continued to say Grand Central.

And just as adamantly, the customers continued to call it The White. It officially became The White

---

This is The Old White Hotel, which served the patrons of White Sulphur Springs between 1858 and 1922. The bronze tablet that commemorates it today was placed near the corner of the piazza.

Where else but to the springs did pamphleteer Edmund Ruffin go to persuade influential southerners to support secession? And who else but Ruffin fired the first cannonade at Fort Sumter?

after the hotel was purchased by the Chesapeake & Ohio in 1910 (railroad men, after all, knew the type of structure that deserved the name Grand Central). By then, the fickle public had changed its tune: no longer was it The White, but The Old White.

Today, a hotel 120 by 450 feet with three floors and a basement does not seem as impressive as it did then. Newspapers even reported that White Sulphur's guest capacity jumped from between 1,000–1,500 at one time to a whopping 3,000–5,000. This seems highly optimistic, unless guests were packed in like sardines, for the total number of rooms in the new hotel was 228.

But in 1858 it was a matter of pride. For a South dependent in so many ways on an industrialized North, it was a pride in local ownership making good. It was a pride in things southern.

As an additional point, the planters who visited White Sulphur could note the economic conditions. For the financial crisis that struck the North in 1857 (in the same month, as it happened, that construction began on the hotel) had little effect on the prices paid for the South's cotton, tobacco and sugar. To planters who had been severely hit by the panics of 1837 and 1847 before it, this fact was another bit of evidence that the South could go it alone.

*O*ther frictions with the North increased attendance at the Virginia springs. Though few southern newspapers played up the 1858 speech of an Illinois lawyer named Abraham Lincoln ("a house divided against itself cannot stand... this government cannot endure permanently half slave and half free"), they gave great prominence to letters from southerners who were annoyed and challenged by

northern abolitionists. And if these provocations were not an organized effort, they occurred so often that they might just as well have been. The *Richmond Dispatch* drew this conclusion: "If people will go among abolitionists and free negroes, they must be prepared for the consequences."

As southerners cut their northern ties, the seasons at White Sulphur became more brilliant—perhaps in unconscious apprehension of the dreary war years ahead.

But changes in spring life were already apparent, many of them brought about by a firebrand pamphleteer whose distinguished scientific researches on fertilizer earned him the title "father of soil chemistry." Edmund Ruffin viewed the world through deep-set eyes that peered from under his shoulder-length white hair. He spent four summers at White Sulphur trying to convert the influential men of the South. "I find myself alone as an avowed disunionist per se," he wrote, "but I avow that opinion upon every occasion." At The White, he found the men who, organized as the Publication Society, were to print his tracts. He obtained a further outlet for his inflammatory gospel after talking to newspaper owner Barnwell Rhett. One day he would seek out Senator Chestnut, on another, it might be Governor McWillie, Judge Hopkins or Judge Withers. And here, perhaps, he met Wilmer McLean of Manassas, Virginia, whose choice in real estate would be so curious a sidelight to the coming conflict.

As the summer of 1859 moved on, a lieutenant colonel in the U.S. Army and his arthritic wife made a visit to a Virginia spring—not this time to White Sulphur, but to Capon Springs, some 200 miles northeast. And it was while his wife was still at the spring that Robert E. Lee was sent to quell a

*Charley Bonaparte drilled
fellow youngsters at White Sulphur
in 1860—and as an adult
organized the force
that is today the Federal
Bureau of Investigation.*

mysterious insurrection at Harpers Ferry, led by one John Brown.

Where Edmund Ruffin had previously been one of few who preached secession, after the capture of John Brown he was one of many. Ruffin, by wheedling the scarlet, white and gray uniform of a Virginia Military Institute cadet, was an up-front observer of Brown's execution. Another who borrowed a uniform to view the hanging was a popular young actor from Richmond who then used the stage name, J. B. Wilkes.

*D*uring the winter, the uproar increased. And when the White Sulphur season began on June 1, 1860, the proprietors had installed a pistol gallery for the convenience and necessity of registered guests. Soon after the season opened, Company F of the Richmond Volunteers arrived for training. Among those who pitched their tents on the brow of Copeland Hill above the spring was Virginia's governor, 57-year-old John Letcher. Not for him this year was The Treadmill he had so often enjoyed; he lived and trained with his men.

There was one less-than-military note, however. Some Richmond belles did traipse up the hill to eat at the officers' mess. But the ladies were being organized into shooting clubs by Edmund Ruffin.

Preoccupations of the elders affected the young, and that year the children made a great game of marching. Often as not, young Charley Bonaparte, great-grandnephew of Napoleon, would be in the lead. (Charley's talent for organization would later lead him to establish the Federal Bureau of Investigation.) Though 1860 was the year that Charley's grandfather, Jerome Napoleon Bonaparte, owner of Baltimore "E" cottage, would sue in the French courts for an inheritance and recognition in the

To the Patriots
—OF—
NorthWestern VIRGINIA!!

WHEREAS—a Convention is to be held in Wheeling on the 11th. of this month, for the avowed purpose of effecting a division of the State, and attaching a portion thereof, as a miserable appendage, to one of the Republican states, or else forming the same into a new, and insignificant Free State: And believing that either change would be ruinous to our property and our social happiness:—We therefore earnestly call upon the people of North-Western Virginia, in their several counties, who still remain loyal to the "Old Dominion," and are opposed to being tacked on to the "TAIL END" of the BLACK REPUBLICAN DESPOTISM! to send Delegates to a convention to be held at Lewisburg, on the first Monday in July next, to enter their solemn PROTEST against this wicked and treasonable scheme; and also to take such action as may then be thought proper, after knowing the result of the Wheeling Convention. If a convention, gotten up as the one to be held at Wheeling has been, has the power to divide the State; then, upon the same supposition, we, in convention, by the same right and power, can annul their acts, or SEPARATE AGAIN FROM THEM!!

Lewisburg, Va. June, 1st. 1861.

*When Virginia seceded from the Union in 1861,
many of its western citizens favored the formation
of a new, free state. Such was not the case
in the White Sulphur Springs area, as this poster makes clear.
Despite these efforts, Greenbrier county was included
when the new state of West Virginia was formed.*

As the "War Between Brothers" approached,
volunteers hastened to enlist.
Some of the Confederates shown above
may well have been among those
who trained on the hills that overlook
White Sulphur Springs during 1860.
The Federals were also active,
as indicated by this assemblage of troops.

Bonaparte line of succession, the members of his family were, as usual, at White Sulphur.

While the militia and its young imitators drilled, the politicians were busy. Vote for Breckenridge! Down with black Republicans! But soon after the White Sulphur season ended, Abraham Lincoln was elected president of the United States. Four days later, South Carolina called for secession, and a unanimous vote followed on December 20. "Hotheads...rejoiced," wrote Douglas Southall Freeman, "as though the division of the Union were as great an act as its creation."

At 4:30 a.m. on April 12, 1861, who but Edmund Ruffin was given the honor of firing the first cannon shot against Fort Sumter. General P. G. T. Beauregard, commander of the southern forces there and a White Sulphur visitor of the future, hailed the 67-year-old Ruffin for "undergoing every fatigue and sharing the hardships at the battery with the youngest."

Beauregard soon met Wilmer McLean, too, for it was from Mrs. McLean's brick farmhouse near Bull Run that he commanded the Confederate forces in the first major battle of the civil war. And McLean's description of the terrain, Beauregard reported, was invaluable. Edmund Ruffin also served there—as a "temporary private."

One of the problems faced by the Confederacy in western Virginia (for there was no state of West Virginia until well along in the war) was its antislavery sentiment. Most of the residents had come southwest from Pennsylvania, not straight west from tidewater Virginia. When Virginia seceded from the Union, leaders from its northwest section refused to accede. Through a series of conventions held in Wheeling, they set up the anti-slavery Restored Government of Virginia. They planned to

Colonel George S. Patton

General William W. Averell

establish a state called Kanawha in their territory, an area that did not include Greenbrier County, which had voted for secession. But later, the boundaries were extended for military reasons to include all counties west of the Allegheny Mountain crest—thus bringing White Sulphur Springs four miles inside the area that became West Virginia in 1863.

*E*ven with the war on, there was an 1861 season at The White—with rates reduced "owing to the embarrassed state of the country." And though most Greenbrier County residents were sympathetic to the Confederacy, the same was not true of The White's room clerks. The notation that followed the name of a Mr. G. Roberts who registered on July 22 termed him a "traitor to the Wheeling Convention."

The season lasted until August 23 (a month short of normal), but even before the close, there were troops at The White. A former Virginia governor, General Henry Wise, marched by on the James River and Kanawha Turnpike in his advance on Charleston. When he thought he was threatened by superior forces, he fell back to White Sulphur. Meanwhile, an independent army under another ex-Virginia-governor-turned-general, John Floyd, arrived at the spring. The conflicts of these old political enemies who met at White Sulphur became so serious that Robert E. Lee, now in command of the Confederate forces, was summoned to mediate.

While Lee was in the area, he first saw the gray four-year-old horse that was to become his favorite mount, Traveller. The steed had been raised at Blue Sulphur Springs, a few miles west of The White. Originally called Jeff Davis, he had been

renamed Greenbrier before Lee purchased him in late '61. The animal's reputation as a "fine traveller" gave him his final name.

Any semblance of normal operations at White Sulphur had by now been suspended, with a Miss Emily Mason in charge of the inactive property. One chronicler gushed: "She not only proved to be the most distinguished Florence Nightingale of the Old Dominion in those strenuous years, but by her tactful management and her potent personality, saved the White Sulphur hotel and surrounding cottages from injury and destruction."

*O*ne moment at which her potent personality would be tested was in August, 1863, during a raid on Confederate positions by General William W. Averell. Though Averell had been ordered to destroy powder and saltpeter works on his route, his objective was to seize the books in the law library at Lewisburg, nine miles west of White Sulphur Springs. The courthouse at Lewisburg, site of the western sessions of the Virginia Court of Appeals, had often provided an afternoon's entertainment to springs visitors who enjoyed the legal oratory.

Averell, after destroying saltpeter operations on Jackson's River near Covington, marched his forces west on the turnpike (now U.S. Highway 60) towards White Sulphur and Lewisburg. At 9:30 a.m. on August 26, they reached the intersection with what is today State Route 15 near the eastern edge of White Sulphur Springs and met a Confederate force marching south. These troops were commanded by Col. George S. Patton, whose grandson and namesake was to make military history during World War II.

The battle that followed has been variously described as the Engagement at Rocky Gap, or as

General David Hunter

Captain Henry A. du Pont

The Battle of Dry Creek, Dry Run, Howard's Creek or White Sulphur Springs. Whatever the name, it was a bloody battle. Averell sent his cavalry against the center, then the right and then the left flanks of Patton's forces, gaining perhaps 400 yards. But counter charges caused him to fall back, and as evening arrived, the lines stood about where they were that morning. Moreover, both sides were running low on ammunition. Averell resumed his charging at daybreak, but was repulsed. Another try at about 10 a.m. was also unsuccessful. Then came a shock; from the direction in which Averell expected reinforcements came more Confederates. He called a retreat, and the Union forces began to march east towards Covington, felling trees as they went, to blockade the turnpike behind them and delay pursuit.

And thus the battle ended. The law books were untouched. Emily Mason had 380 casualties to care for.

Averell himself finally got to White Sulphur on June 3, 1864, with a force of Union troops marching east from Charleston to join General David Hunter in his advance in the Shenandoah Valley. The meeting took place at Staunton, and the combined force, after burning much of the city of Lexington, moved south towards Lynchburg. As Hunter mounted his attack, he discovered that reinforcements had joined the battle. They were troops commanded by General Jubal Early, detached from General Lee's forces further east. Suddenly unsure of himself, Hunter decided to retreat. And though the sounder move would have been to return along the Shenandoah as he came, he chose to go west over the James River and Kanawha Pike.

This choice was to give White Sulphur its last real moment in Civil War history. Hunter, whose forces included a Colonel Rutherford B. Hayes and a Captain William McKinley, arrived at the spring on Friday, June 24. After an inspection of the grounds, Hunter resolved to set fire to the buildings upon departure. Much of our information on this visit comes from a memoir published in 1925 by Henry Algernon du Pont of Winterthur, Delaware, son of the munitions maker who supplied much of the Union's powder during the war. Though the 25-year-old du Pont, a future winner of the Congressional Medal of Honor, was only a captain, he had been Hunter's chief of artillery for exactly one month.

"I reported to General Hunter about noon [he wrote] and made inquiry as to the hour for beginning the march... I remarked, as I was about to depart, 'General, I hear that you intend to burn the buildings here when we leave.' He replied, 'Yes, I intend to burn them all down.' After a short pause, I said, 'Don't you think, General, that the burning of these structures would be a military mistake?' This seemed to arouse him, and, raising his voice a little, he at once asked, 'What do you mean, Captain, by that inquiry?' Looking him squarely in the eyes, my response was as follows: 'I mean this, General—if we have later to occupy and hold this country, the White Sulphur Springs will be the natural point for our principal station, as so many roads converge here. Such being the case, the buildings as they stand would furnish excellent winter quarters for at least a brigade of troops.' He said nothing but looked at me with some suspicion, I thought. In a few seconds, however, his expression changed and he quietly remarked, 'Well, I had

not thought of that,' whereupon he instantly called his orderly and sent for the adjutant-general to report forthwith. Upon the arrival of this officer, Hunter said at once, 'Colonel, I have changed my mind about burning the buildings here. Don't issue the order.'"

Though Hunter's retreat to the West was to give Jubal Early a free passage up the Shenandoah Valley to harass the Federals near Washington, the Union's superior numbers and supplies, as the weeks and months went on, would take their inevitable toll. In September and October, Early's 14,000 men were badly defeated by 40,000 under Sheridan. Further south, as Hood attempted to cut Union communications between Atlanta and Tennessee, Sherman began his march to the sea, and then went on up the coast. Grant's well-fed and well-reinforced Army of the Potomac became ever stronger than Lee's poorly-supplied Army of Northern Virginia. Finally, in the forlorn hope of joining forces in North Carolina with Johnston, came Lee's final retreat from Richmond and Petersburg toward Appomattox Court House.

The surrender was signed on April 9, 1865—in a red brick house purchased in 1862 by a man fleeing the battlegrounds of northern Virginia, our old friend Wilmer McLean. This moment of sorrow for the South occurred on Palm Sunday; the North's sorrow came five days later. For it was on Good Friday that John Wilkes Booth, the actor who had observed the execution of John Brown, assassinated Abraham Lincoln.

Thus it ended, but for a postscript. Two months later in a farmhouse near Amelia, the firebrand-persuader of White Sulphur Springs, Edmund Ruffin, considered the bitter results. After bathing and putting on clean clothes, he sat down, put a loaded musket in his mouth and, leaning back, struck the trigger with a hickory stick.

One of the war's coincidences revolved about Wilmer McLean,
for his farmhouse near Bull Run (center picture)
was used by the southern command during the battle.
McLean soon sold out and moved his family south
—to Appomattox Court House, where the
final armistice was signed in the parlor of his new home.

LEE VISITS THE SPRINGS

"Many a young Southerner owed
his acquaintance with the belle of the season
to General Lee's
stately presentation."

Slowly, painfully, but inevitably, southern life began once more. Soldiers returned home, and started a late plowing to plant what they could for the winter ahead. To the men in ragged gray who straggled back to Greenbrier County, things went easier than with their fellow soldiers across the Allegheny ridge, for the free state of West Virginia escaped the reconstruction.

The White Sulphur properties were heavily damaged though still basically sound, and a new joint stock company was formed by George L. Peyton and his brothers to lease the springs and operate the hotel. Cleaning, painting and fixing went on apace. The steps to many Alabama, Paradise and Baltimore Cottages had rotted, so they were replaced. The White's furniture was repaired and new drapes and mirrors were ordered for the ballroom. A race track was opened, and Howard's Creek was dammed into an artificial lake. Atop the spring house, Hygeia had been shot away, so they painted over the vacant spot. (Today's statue of Hebe, Cupbearer to the gods and Goddess of Youth, was added some years later.)

The White opened its doors on June 18, 1867, and though the *Richmond Dispatch* reported that "we cannot expect to see there the society that once gave life and gayety and grace to that incomparably delightful summer resort," the paper was wrong. For the man who would change it all arrived in late afternoon on July 24.

Except for his size 4½ C riding boots, the erect rider was a man in gray—the wide-brimmed hat, hair, beard, the old army coat, riding gauntlets and

horse. As a newspaper correspondent observed, one could almost have taken him for a farmer.

The man was Robert E. Lee, former superintendent at West Point and, of course, the ex-commander of the Army of Northern Virginia. Lee was president of Washington College (the Washington and Lee University of today).

This was the first of the visits to White Sulphur Springs he planned for the summers of 1867 to 1870. But this visit, unlike his succeeding ones, was not of his own choosing, for though he had taken his wife to Capon Springs and the Rockbridge Baths, among others, in attempting to alleviate her rheumatism, none seemed of any help. So he brought her to White Sulphur "merely on the ground, I believe, that she has never tried those waters, and therefore, they might be of service to her." The atmosphere of White Sulphur appealed to him, for he returned with members of his family in 1868 and 1869. And the visit he planned for 1870 was so nearly certain that he wrote White Sulphur's proprietors exactly when to expect him.

On that afternoon of July 24, 1867, the first of the Lee party to arrive were the general and a friend from the college—apparently Professor James J. White—who had made the journey by horseback. Soon came the coach that held Mrs. Lee, son Custis, daughter Agnes, her friend, Mary Pendleton, and Mrs. Lee's maid, Milly Howard. There were strangers in the stagecoach, for though it had been reserved for the Lee party, the general had offered places to some of those whose overcrowded coaches had left Covington at the same time. For the first night, at least, they stayed in The White, with General and Mrs. Lee in room 116, but soon they moved to Baltimore "G" cottage. Mrs. Lee had her meals sent to the cottage; the rest of the party ate in the main dining room at a table shared with W. W. Corcoran, the banker.

There was a question on the first evening as to how Lee should be greeted. The guests, for fear of embarrassing him, had already deferred the usual salutation to an honored visitor—driving their carriages out several miles to accompany the personage to the gates. But while the discussion was going on, Lee entered. Almost as one, the crowd stood up, lapsing into respectful silence until he had taken his seat. When assured by this incident that there would be no effusive demonstrations, he made regular visits to the hotel's parlor after each meal, taking his place in The Treadmill of old.

His young friend Christiana Bond wrote that "everyone took part in a promenade up and down the great uncarpeted space, not usually in couples but in lines of three or four. Here introductions took place, here engagements were made, and this was the stranger's opportunity to be absorbed into the strenuous stream of life. It was only the old or the feeble who sat along the walls, unless a rare ostracism left the objectionable stranger stranded on the shore.

"Groups of young men, the newcomers, gathered about the doors to await fortunate opportunities, and were soon joined to some one of the constantly changing lines. It was a gay, informal scene, bewildering to the lookers-on. There was a graceful rhythm in the motion, as groups and couples threaded the winding maze, and there was harmony of sound in the mingling of tuneful Southern voices.

"The influence of General Lee was always present in these promenades. It was his time to dispense the kindly courtesies which made him the presiding genius of the place. He loved young people, especially young girls, for, to confess the truth, the young men were not thoroughly at ease with him; he seemed to test them with an Ithuriel spear, and they were inclined to shrink from the lofty standard he maintained.

"He loved to see the girls surrounded by cavaliers and merry in the dance, and many a young Southerner owed his acquaintance with the belle of the season to General Lee's stately presentation. The keen, kindly eye was always alert lest some one should fail to share in the general happiness." (In this last comment, Miss Bond shows a different viewpoint from that of R. E. Lee, Jr., who wrote that whenever his father appeared in parlor or ball-room, "he was the center of attraction, and in vain the young men tried to engage the attention of the young ladies when General Lee was present.")

Lee's "quiet influence, subtle and unacknowledged, permeated the throng and welded it into a gracious community regardful of mutual needs and pleasures... He was the interested observer, too, of many incipient love affairs. He had the Southerner's deference for woman, and the Southerner's respect for her right of flirtation. It was a man's privilege to 'court' and the woman's right to 'discard'—old-fashioned words now, but common enough in those more chivalric days."

As a token of friendship, Lee gave Miss Bond a velvet watch case embroidered with gold thread. "It was under my pillow every night during the war when I *had* a pillow," said the general. "Now let it be under yours."

During Lee's visit, Castello, Barnum and Van Amburgh's Great Show came to the town of White Sulphur Springs and the circus manager sent him free passes. These he refused, but purchased tickets for many of his young friends, who sat in seats draped in Confederate red and white. When they returned, Lee invited them up on his cottage veranda to share a sixty-pound watermelon, sent him by express all the way from Mobile, Alabama.

In a letter written to R. E. Lee, Jr., on August 5, he promised to get "Agnes or your mother to tell you what occurs at the Springs. There are some 500 people here, very pleasant and kind, but most of my time is passed alone with Traveller in the mountains."

And sometimes, it was not quite so alone. One day, two female White Sulphur guests set out on an often-postponed walk on a steep trail to the top of Kate's Mountain. "Part of the ascent," one wrote, "lay through a very deep wood and the road was seldom traveled. It was here, in the loneliest part, that we heard behind us the sound of horse's hoofs and saw the well-known form of Traveller." Lee dismounted, doffed his hat and said, "I overheard you this morning planning to climb the mountain, and I could not suffer you to go unattended. With your permission I will accompany you." He urged each lady to mount Traveller, and when both declined, he joined them in the walk to the summit, "beguiling the way with kindly talk." Only when they had returned to within sight of The White did he again mount Traveller

This famous photograph celebrates the 1868 season at White Sulphur Springs. Seated, from left, are Blacque-Bey, ambassador from Turkey, General Robert E. Lee, George Peabody, W. W. Corcoran and Judge James Lyons of Richmond. Eight former Confederate Army officers are shown in the second row; from left, Generals Conner, Gary, Magruder, Lilley, Beauregard, Lawton, Wise and Brent.

and ride off. There was good reason for Lee's concern, for only a few days before, the same two had gotten lost in the hills while searching for a good spot to view the sunset. As they finally straggled back to the hotel, they met a party organized to search for them. Some congratulated them on a safe return, but Lee pointed out that their search for "selfish enjoyment" had caused their relatives some anxious moments.

When an invalid patient from Pennsylvania remarked to Dr. Moorman that she was sorry not to be up and about so that she could meet Lee, the word was passed, and the next day Lee visited her room, "and sat sometime with the lady to her great gratification."

Another visitor from Pennsylvania was that state's wartime governor, Andrew G. Curtin. One evening when Lee arrived in the parlor, he saw the Curtins seated somewhat apart from the other guests. When Lee asked his young acquaintances

if they had welcomed the newcomers, he received evasive answers, for, quite frankly, they thought that the northerners had come to gloat over the South's distress. Lee was not willing to have the situation continue.

"I have tried in vain," he said as he stood up, "to find any lady who has made acquaintance with the party and is able to present me. I shall now introduce myself, and shall be glad to present any of you who will accompany me." There was a pause, and finally it was Christiana Bond who said, "I will go, General Lee, under your orders."

"Not under my orders," he replied, "but it will gratify me deeply to have your assistance."

And so, with all eyes upon them, the general and his 22-year-old companion started across the ballroom floor. Under the brilliant chandelier he paused, telling her that he regretted young southerners showing such bitterness. "But General Lee," she asked, "did you never feel resentment towards the North?" He replied, earnestly: "I believe I may

say, looking into my own heart, and speaking as in the presence of God, that I have never known one moment of bitterness or resentment." He paused, but kept Miss Bond in the focus of his brown, almost black, eyes. "When you go home, I want you to take a message to your young friends. Tell them from me that it is unworthy of them as women, and especially as Christian women, to cherish feelings of resentment against the North. Tell them that it grieves me inexpressibly to know that such a state of things exists, and that I implore them to do their part to heal our country's wounds."

They moved on across the floor toward the Curtins, where Lee presented himself and his young friend. They were offered and accepted seats, conversing for some minutes. From that time on, though some restraint was still shown, southerners and northerners at White Sulphur at least talked to one another.

One evening later that summer, as Lee was again urging his belles to forget their bitterness, a pugnacious one spit out, "Well, General Lee, they say General Grant is coming here next week; what will you do then?" Ignoring the gasps from others at the thoughtlessness of this riposte, Lee quietly replied, "If General Grant comes I shall welcome him to my home, show him all the courtesy which is due from one gentleman to another, and try to do everything in my power to make his stay here agreeable." Whether Grant ever planned an 1867 trip, we do not know (he did come to White Sulphur in 1874). But at the only post-Appomattox confrontation of the two generals, held in Washington on May 1, 1869, Lee was accompanied to the White House by Mr. and Mrs. Samuel Tagart of Baltimore, owners of a White Sulphur cottage,

whom he had first met on a visit to the spring.

The Lees concluded their visit to White Sulphur on August 15, at a time when the Peyton brothers' crowd had reached 700, its peak for the season.

For 1868, the Peytons had further plans. Seeing the hit that General Lee had made the year before, they invited many other former Confederate generals and civilian officials to join him at The White. General Beauregard came, as did Generals Echols and Johnston, former Vice-President Stephens, and many others. And because there were so many influential southerners in attendance, a Union general and northern Democrat, W. S. Rosecrans, also showed up.

With a presidential election that November, it was a political summer at The White. People were discussing how best to elect the Democratic candidate Horatio Seymour over Republican U. S. Grant. Rosecrans was one of the managers of Seymour's campaign, and hoped to counteract the Republican claim that Seymour would let the South continue as though no war had occurred.

Rosecrans went to Lee and asked him to affirm the South's loyalty to the Union. But Lee demurred, for ever since the war he had specifically avoided any discussion of politics—so rigorously that Colonel John Mosby once remarked that Lee was snubbing his old compatriots. Instead, Lee suggested Rosecrans talk with a cross section of influential southerners at the spring, and organized such a meeting. Most of those who spoke with Rosecrans in Lee's cottage said that, following the verdict of battle, they now supported the Washington government and had every intention of

General W. S. Rosecrans

Miss Christiana Bond

treating the Negroes fairly. When Rosecrans asked that this be put in writing, Lee asked Alexander H. H. Stuart to draft a statement. Stuart wrote:

"...Whatever opinions may have prevailed in the past with regard to African slavery or the right of a State to secede from the Union, we believe we express the almost unanimous judgment of the Southern people when we declare that they consider these questions were decided by the war, and that it is their intention in good faith to abide by that decision... If their action in these particulars had been met in a spirit of frankness and cordiality, we believe that, ere this, old irritations would have passed away...

"The important fact that the two races are, under existing circumstances, necessary to each other is gradually becoming apparent to both, and we believe that but for malign influences exerted to stir up the passions of the negroes, the relations of the two races would soon adjust themselves on a basis of mutual kindness and advantage...

"The great want of the South is peace. The people...ask a restoration of their rights under the Constitution... Above all, they would appeal to their countrymen for the re-establishment of the right of self-government. Establish these on a firm basis, and we can safely promise, on behalf of the Southern people, that they will faithfully obey the Constitution and laws of the United States, treat the negro populations with kindness and humanity and fulfil every duty incumbent on peaceful citizens, loyal to the Constitution of their country."

Lee read Stuart's text and said, "Mr. Stuart, there is one word I would like to strike out if you have no objection. You have used the word *malign*. I think that is rather a harsh word, and"—he

smiled—"I never did like adjectives." Stuart erased the word, Lee signed, and so did 31 others who were then at the spring. The White Sulphur Manifesto had come into being.

Two days later, Lee wrote his son: "The place looks beautiful—the belles very handsome, and the beaux very happy. All are gay, and only I solitary. I am all alone. There was a grand fancy masked ball last night. The room was overflowing, the music good, as much spring in the boards as in the conversation, and the German continued 'til two o'clock this morning."

The dance to which Lee referred was the first of the season's two costume balls. Both were smashingly successful, though it took some doing to resew the patchwork costumes of the first into new disguises for the second. Enough diamonds had been resurrected from wartime burial beneath the magnolia trees that one spoilsport spinster lamented, "Oh that I had the jewels and laces to sell for the poor of dear suffering Carolina!"

But hers was a voice crying in the wilderness. More typical was this 1868 newspaper report:

"Soft music floats on the air, and beauty haunts the bowers and the groves. But if you will risk the loss of your senses, visit the magnificent ball-room, perhaps the finest in the world—'where youth and pleasure meet, to chase the glowing hours with flying feet.'

"There you will behold every style of beauty in which our wide-spread country exults—the golden locks and azure eyes of the northern blonde, and the raven locks and black eyes of the southern brunette. But view them in motion, as 'on gossamer pinions they float through the air' so buoyant, so sylph-like, that you do not realize that they are things of earth till, in the whirling mazes of the dance, you catch a glimpse of a foot and ankle."

*B*ut if 1868 was the year of the great social revival, 1869 was the year of good food and drink. For the Peytons took great pride in the table they set. One of the features was beef—from a 4,000 pound shorthorn steer that had been exhibited at the nearby Lewisburg fair. The price paid was $500, something over 12¢ a pound, at a time that the best beef sold for 7¼¢. (By contrast, in 1956 when The Greenbrier bought the purebred shorthorn Troubadour, grand champion steer at the International Livestock Exposition, it paid $20.50 a pound.)

The 1869 menu was chosen with care. Featured, in addition to ribs of beef, were chicken livers en brochette, bœuf à la mode, saddles of venison and lamb—and, for southern traditionalists, middling and greens.

*A*nd to bring the people directly to this scene of social and gastronomic splendor: enter the early woodburning locomotives of the Chesapeake and Ohio Railroad. The first train from Richmond arrived on July 1, 1869.

The coming of the railroad was a triumph for White Sulphur. Though it had always been the largest of the fifteen commercially operated springs, this cemented its triumph. The White was the only one on the main railroad line.

The Chesapeake and Ohio Rail*way** of today traces one chain of its corporate history back to 1785 and a canal company headed by George Washington. Today, White Sulphur might be considerably different had this organization's plans been realized. During the 1850's, it blueprinted a remarkable canal tunnel; 50 feet wide, 30 feet high and nine miles long, through the Allegheny ridge —a tunnel that would have gone several hundred feet under White Sulphur Springs. The railroad that was actually built along the property represents another portion of the C&O ancestry, one that dates back to the Louisa Railroad of 1836, its successor, the Virginia Central Railroad, and the later-chartered Covington and Ohio Railroad.

Agitation for a railroad to White Sulphur had gone on for many years. This 1852 comment of a

Lewisburg newspaper, *The Western Era*, was typical: With a railroad, "hundreds drawn by its romantic and beautiful scenery, shaking the dust of the city from their garments and its cares and dissipation from their minds, would flock thither." But by the Civil War's start, the rails reached only a bit west of Clifton Forge, though masonry was completed to Covington, and a right of way had been graded, and tunnel sites chosen as far as White Sulphur. Soon after the war ended, the Virginia and West Virginia legislatures set up commissions to speed construction to the Ohio River. In July, 1867, a railroad conference was held at The White to raise money, and construction began once again. There were still some financial problems, for by mid-1869, when the trains from Richmond reached The White over a temporary roadbed, more money was needed to complete even the permanent tunnels below those tracks. The Connecticut financier Collis P. Huntington became interested in the line as part of his planned coast-to-coast railroad chain. He arranged for new funds, and was named president near the end of 1869. Four years later, the last spike was driven, joining Chesapeake Bay to the Ohio by rail—via White Sulphur Springs.

*I*f freight and express shippers had their plans for the railroad, so did the belles. At last, they could bring *all* the gowns they wanted! So the satchels, reticules, bonnet boxes, and those backbreakingly heavy northern devices known as Saratoga trunks arrived in ever greater numbers.

And what costumes they wore! A belle could wear one gown at breakfast, a second for the morning cotillion, a third for the noontime "dinner," a fourth for the afternoon concert, and one or two more for supper, The Treadmill and a night of dancing.

The big costume dance of the 1869 season was the Peabody Ball, named for the Boston and London philanthropist who had given $3,500,000 to the Fund for Southern Education—a cause, he told a White Sulphur friend, that "lies very close to my heart."

Peabody came to White Sulphur to try its waters, and stayed for four or five weeks. He was not well, and spent most of his time in his room. Occasionally he went for short walks or for carriage drives. On one of the latter, he said to his servant: "John, pay the man before we start." The servant asked the charges, and the carriageman told him five

---

* In 1878, the Chesapeake and Ohio Railroad was reorganized as the Chesapeake and Ohio Railway.

dollars. The millionaire overheard this, and said "That is too much, sir, three dollars is enough, and if you do not take that, I will get out immediately." The driver took it, and the ride was on.

The dance in Peabody's honor threw the *Richmond Whig* into ecstasy: "Two thousand people, the peers of the most gifted, distinguished and gentle-blooded to be found in either section of our vast country...never has there been brought together a crowd of fair women and brave men which represented more largely the refined beauty, grace, worth and intellect of our country than that which did honor to Mr. Peabody."

Almost sixty of the ladies drew newspaper paragraphs praising them for velvet, silk and satin costumes, loaded with diamonds, sapphires and rubies. The only exception was Agnes Lee, the general's daughter. The *Whig* noted that she appeared in "simple white tarletan." A champagne supper was served at eleven, and at midnight the dance began again. Only at three did those who crowded both the Old White's ballroom and dining room finally make their way to bed, stepping past the cots placed in the hall for the roomless many. Still others made their way to the nearby C&O depot for the 4:30 a.m. Richmond express. The reporters, with hyperbole in heart and glowing adjective in mind sat down in the coaches to write their stories. They generally managed to forget that George Peabody was too sick to stir from his bed.

*B*ut though the patriarchs gathered to talk and be photographed, it was not a year for older men. Peabody died that November, and Lee would "strike his tent" eleven months later. Lee's comment on the 1869 season was that he "should prefer more quiet." He was back at his home in Lexington, Virginia, before the end of August, to leave it only three times before his death. The first of these trips was his grand goodbye, a two-month tour through much of the South—a journey that has but one footnote to this story of the springs. While at a reception in Augusta, Georgia, 13-year-old Thomas Wilson squeezed his way through the crowds to stand for a moment next to the general, looking up into his face. Thomas was a future visitor to White Sulphur; he became better known by his middle name, Woodrow.

On Lee's second trip, he visited Baltimore and his friends from the springs, the Tagarts. His third journey was the one that almost included a farewell to White Sulphur. It began with a letter from his ever-alert friends, the Peytons. Jefferson Davis had arrived at White Sulphur unexpectedly on July 30, and the Peytons wrote Lee, inviting him to join his former commander-in-chief.

"It would give me great pleasure," Lee responded, "to see Mr. Davis, as well as the other friends now at the White Sulphur, among whom I always number yourselves. I will, therefore, if nothing prevents, be there about the middle of next week... As far as I can judge, I shall be able to leave here Tuesday morning, 9th inst., and reach the W.S. that evening on the 10½ train." But on Monday the eighth, having heard from the Peytons that Davis had already left White Sulphur, Lee wrote that his physicians thought he should take advantage of some warm, dry weather to test a new hot-bath treatment. "If I can accomplish a visit after trying the baths...it will give me great pleasure to do so, for I always enjoy the W. S. very much."

*I*t was not to be. Lee's health got worse instead of better. His hair was now white, his shoulders were no longer ramrod straight, his walk was slow. On September 28, he walked hatless through chilling rain to attend a meeting of church vestrymen. It was still raining as he walked home. When Mrs. Lee saw him she remarked that he looked chilled. "Thank you, I am warmly clothed," he replied. But when he sat down at the supper table and tried to say grace, he could not speak. After calling the doctor, the family brought a bed downstairs for him. And there he lay.

To the superstitious, there were omens. A picture of him fell down from the wall. A flash flood that swept through Lexington destroyed a shipment of coffins—all but one. There were several evenings with bright displays of northern lights, and one neighbor quoted these lines of a Scottish poem to a friend:
"All night long the northern streamers Shoot across the trembling sky: Fearful lights, that never beckon Save when kings or heroes die."

For days Lee seemed to improve, but on October 10, life began to ebb. On the morning of the twelfth, at a few minutes after nine, he received a celestial marching order.

"Strike the tent," he said firmly. It was his prompt and last reply.

THE MYSTIQUE OF THE BELLES

*"The Lord made the White Sulphur Springs
and then the Southern girl,
and rested,
satisfied with His work."*

The Peytons were good for the springs, and the springs were good for the Peytons. By 1873, George Peyton was operating not only White Sulphur but the Sweet Chalybeate Springs as well. His brother, C.S. Peyton, was proprietor at both Salt Sulphur and Red Sulphur. The Peytons now had charge of well over a third of all accommodations at the fifteen springs of the Virginias.

Frankly, though belles and beaux flocked to White Sulphur, such diversification was necessary in the "poor seventies." For the White Sulphur Springs Company, from whom the Peytons were leasing, was in serious financial trouble.

"We find the grass unmowed," wrote Mary B. Dodge in *Lippincott's Magazine*, "except by trampling feet; the gravel paths unweeded; steps leading into once favored summer-houses falling to decay; everything evincing taste in the original design, but unkempt as a beggar child's profuse and ringleted hair. The enigma is solved in a statement that the present proprietors have leased the property from a company who refuse to do anything toward repairs. The term has nearly expired...

"Yet nobody talks of the discomfort, nobody appears to feel it. Has not Fashion lifted each and all above the meanness of a comment on such petty details?... Ah! Fashion is kind or cruel as she wantonly pleases, and she pleases to be madly in love with the White Sulphur."

But as Fashion smiled, Bankers frowned, and the White Sulphur Springs Company continued to have monetary problems. In 1879, a wealthy cattle farmer and salt baron named William A. Stuart

foreclosed on the company's $300,000 first mortgage. Upon receiving full title in 1882, he formed the new Greenbrier White Sulphur Springs Company, which sold bonds to finance further improvements. One of his plans was to expand The White from its original 450-by-120-foot size into a hotel 450 feet in each direction. (As a local paper remarked, three times around the piazza and you'd walk a mile.) Stuart did build the 450-foot wing on the west side. He put in a racing track (the previous one had fallen into disuse), built a new kitchen wing and hired Adolf Zetelle, former chef to Napoleon III, at $10 per day to operate it. But he never got his four-square hotel.

By the late eighties, Stuart was also in trouble. And history once again repeated, for he was bailed out by another wealthy guest, Baltimore blueblood Henry Grover "Hal" Dulany. But these loans had reached $250,000 by 1888, so Dulany foreclosed. It was his estate that finally sold the property to the Chesapeake & Ohio in 1910—on its second try. The first, soon after Dulany's death, had failed.

In 1888, a syndicate headed by J. P. Morgan and the Vanderbilts had bought out Collis P. Huntington's interest in the C&O. They installed a Bostonian, M. E. Ingalls, as the line's new president. Ingalls fell in love with the White Sulphur area, and rented a farm a few miles from the spring. His family, in the words of Perceval Reniers, "at once bounced into social leadership from a springboard of railroad money, bouncing from there into springs ownership."

Ingalls, with Morgan and other members of the syndicate, tried, first of all, to purchase White Sulphur Springs. At this point, accounts diverge. Ingalls' son wrote that an option was obtained on the spring, but before it could be closed, one of the

---

"White Sulphur is the dancingest place,"
wrote one visitor near the turn of the century.
Souvenir ribbons were all the rage.

syndics who stayed overnight at the Ingalls farm found his white shoes completely covered with mildew. Thus he vetoed purchase of any property in an area where such a calamity could occur. By another story, the Dulany trustees scuttled it all by demanding cash instead of another set of long-term bonds. In any case, the syndicate turned around and bought the Hot, Warm, and Healing Springs, rechristening their purchase The Homestead. Authorizing their railroad to build a spur from its main line, they began to promote their own resort. Next, as one historian wrote, they "curtailed the train service to White Sulphur and, in the vernacular, damn near ruined it." Indeed, The White did not open its doors in 1894—the only year, except those due to the Civil and Second World Wars that White Sulphur Springs did not welcome its public.

Ten years after Ingalls retired as C&O president —and, one must assume, some time after the mildew-prone financier had moved on to figuratively greener pastures—the railroad bought the spring at the behest of Edwin Hawley, then the major C&O stockholder, causing one observer to remark:

"There is one among us today from the North who is moved with the sweetness and the beauty and the romance of the cavaliers and beautiful women of the old place, and he proposes to touch with his golden wand The Old White to bring back its wonderful life."

*A*nd The Old White *had* seen sweetness, beauty and romance, cavaliers and beautiful women. For in the years since the war, southern belledom reached its pinnacle.

"Someone inclined to speak very plainly once said: 'The Lord made the White Sulphur Springs and then the Southern girl, and rested, satisfied with His work.'" This apt, though slightly sacrilegious, hyperbole appeared in a Springfield, Massachusetts, newspaper in 1889. It was typical of what even Yankees were saying about The Old White and its belles.

There was Mary Triplett, over whose hand was fought the last duel ever staged in the Virginias. A woman with a face like a Watteau painting, she was the "unrivalled beauty" of them all, as *The World* advised. The only problem was that though she had become engaged to one John Mordecai, it had not yet been publicly announced. One evening, hot-headed Page McCarty repeatedly invited her to dance with him. Mary, after refusing several times, finally consented, feeling that this would be less conspicuous than to decline once more. The dance over, she curtly moved away, refusing another. McCarty was insulted, and vowed revenge. He sent off a poem to the papers, and it was promptly printed:

"When Mary's queenly form I press
In Strauss' latest waltz,
Her lips I might as well caress
Although those lips be false."

Uproar followed, for in those halcyon days one did not speak lightly of pressing queenly forms, let alone of caressing lips. In full style, Mordecai and McCarty dueled at dawn, and Mordecai received a fatal bullet in his stomach. Did McCarty claim his prize? No, he was so shaken by it all that he died a bachelor. And Mary? She soon married Philip Haxall, who was in textiles, and came back to The Old White for many years.

There was Mattie Ould, whose bon mot, "grace, wit, and beauty make a fair Triplett," was to appear on her chief rival's tombstone. Mattie was an

A group of Old White belles and beaux pause for a portrait on the lawn.

Champagne and a photograph to celebrate the day at White Sulphur Springs.

Off to a "tally-ho picnic"—with, perhaps, a stop to watch the golfers.

Miss Mattie Ould.

Miss May Handy.

Miss Mary Triplett.

After their morning glass of sulphur water, the girls pose by the bridge.

When Charles Dana Gibson first saw Irene Langhorne
she was seated at the piano singing.
He recalled that it sounded as if a cherubim choir sang along.

unusual belle, for she let her wit and intellect show. As a youngster wakened from a doze on the shoulder of a General Young, she remarked that she was "just trying an Ould head on Young shoulders."

When a doting gaffer named Page rushed to pick up her dropped glove before the nearest beau could do the job, he presented it and said,

"If from your glove you take the letter "G,"
Your glove is love and that I bear for thee."
At once she shot back:
"If from your name you take the letter "P,"
Your Page is age; that will not do for me."

She had a million of 'em. To rid herself of a nuisance named Pace, she spoke of "ill weeds that grow apace." Asked if she would marry a Mr. Wise or a Mr. Morrison, she replied, "Oh, hasten, sinner, to be wise; stay not for tomorrow's sun."

But then, in an act for which her father, Judge Ould, never forgave her, she eloped. In mid-August, and with an editor! While waiting for their new home to be built (for this editor had money, if little social standing), they lived in luxuriously furnished rooms—but with a staircase that she said was "just wide enough for a coffin." It may have been prophetic, for Mattie died in childbirth.

There was May Handy, stepsister to Mattie. She was always beautiful, elegant, and a lady. She never looked tired, or had a hair on her head out of place. "I doubt if she ever allowed herself any emotion," one acquaintance wrote. But another, who went out of the way each day to watch her walk by, was kinder: "We were always the recipient of that angelic smile which transformed a perfect face into one of seraphic loveliness."

And there were more. Lizzie Cabell, Sallie Watson Montague, Lillie Norton, Nellie Hazeltine,

Page Aylett (a great-great-great-granddaughter of Patrick Henry), to name but a few.

And then there was Irene Langhorne. Though it was her sister Nancy who would gain the most fame (she became Lady Astor and once told Winston Churchill, "If I were your wife, I should flavor your coffee with arsenic"; growled he: "And were I your husband, I should drink it"), Irene was the belle of them all.

Irene's belledom did not begin with a planned debut. She was sitting with other onlookers in one of the deep window bays of The Old White's ballroom. William Wright of Philadelphia came over between dances and said, "How old are you, Irene?" "Sixteen," she answered. "Then it's time you were out." He lifted her down and they danced. And as she was later to recall, "I loved it, loved it, loved it." Soon thereafter, she met and married Charles Dana Gibson—and became the archetype of his famous Gibson Girl.

*B*ut belledom was going awry. There was Bettina Ordway Padelford. She publicly displayed the transparent Egyptian lingerie she purchased at Philadelphia's Centennial Exposition, and when a newspaper editorial warned her not to catch cold, her career was launched. At White Sulphur one evening that summer, the talk turned to drinking champagne from a lady's slipper. "It's an old custom at Polish weddings," someone remarked. Hal Dulany insisted he'd never try it, but George Morris said it depended on the lady. And he, of course, could depend on Bettina. As she later recalled, "It struck me just then to do something shocking." She took her slipper off and handed it to young Morris. "There's your challenge." He tried to back down, but the others at the table wouldn't leave

Golf was played near White Sulphur Springs in 1884, when five Scotsmen imported the sticks and gutta percha balls from their native land. They held an annual tournament and in 1888 awarded this Challenge Medal.

him alone. So he took the slipper, poured the champagne from his glass into it, and quickly drank it down. Slipper drinking became a social craze elsewhere, but not at White Sulphur. Snapped Major William Hale: "It almost demolished the moral and social structure of the famous resort." Morris got out while the getting was good— on the 4:30 a.m. train that very morning. And though he was to become famous as a state senator and a judge, he, like the unfortunate Page McCarty years before, was never to marry.

Not so Bettina. Before she was done, she married seven times, mostly from the rosters of the stage and vaudeville troupes with which she soon began to perform.

There was Minnie Anderson, who, though married to one William Allen, kept flirting with all comers. When her advances were rejected by a lawyer, she retaliated by publishing his notes to her as "The Love Letters of a Liar." (His only riposte was to print a poem which concluded: "Thank God that I lost you, Bonny Lorraine.") She went off to Rhode Island to become a newspaper correspondent.

There was Alva Smith. She married William K. Vanderbilt and went off to Rhode Island to become an architect, the first woman ever elected to the American Institute of Architects. Alva divorced her Vanderbilt and married O. H. P. Belmont. She was a feminist who used to bicycle in bloomers, and once advised a fellow suffragette, "Brace up, my dear. Just pray to God. *She* will help you."

Yes, belledom was no longer the same. The girls rode their horses astride, not sidesaddle. No longer were they playing tennis in floor-length costumes. And horrors, they were even going to mixed parties in the swimming pool. If James Branch Cabell's

"Jurgen," a thinly disguised tale of the Rockbridge Alum Spring, can be credited, there were less innocent pleasures. But as one defender of belledom's virtue put it:

"The adventures of Jurgen, as all the world knows, are out of a wanton imagination."

One day during the 1884 season, White Sulphur belles and beaux returning from a "tally-ho picnic" stopped at a nearby farm for a moment to watch five enthusiasts play a sport they had imported from Scotland. The game was golf, and it was being played on a nine-hole course on the estate of Russell W. Montague.* The picnicking White Sulphurites watched in silence as the golfers played several holes. Their verdict was "insanity." "I did play marbles when I was a kid," commented one, "but, by gad, this is the first time I've seen men play!" They rode back to the springs, chuckling over this Scots' idiosyncrasy.

There were other changes. During the eighties, the American Medical Association held meetings at White Sulphur. Railroad officials were to gather there before the turn of the century. Lawyers, who had often talked to one another at the springs, found their meetings were becoming more formal.

Physical changes took place. First the White Sulphur estate was lighted with acetylene lamps, and then electricity. A telegraph line came in, followed by the telephone. In 1900 the first horseless carriage arrived at White Sulphur—by rail, in a C&O freight car. A new era was about to begin.

* "There seems no doubt," wrote the assistant executive secretary of the U.S. Golf Association in 1951, "that Montague and four other gentlemen there organized the first full-fledged golf club in the United States. They had a nine-hole course on the Oakhurst estate and annually played for the Oakhurst medal."

TWO WARS AND AN INTERLUDE

"Money, not tradition, made it a heady era
...for this southern watering spot
had become a national society resort."

*I*t was an age of conspicuous affluence. For these were times when Andrew Carnegie's $23 million a year in take-home pay was entirely free from income taxes; when J. P. Morgan would advise a prospective yacht owner that if he had to consider costs, he really couldn't afford a yacht; when George F. Baker hired Albert Bigelow Paine to write his biography—and had exactly six copies printed as gifts to members of his family. For the affluent, these were the good old days.

At White Sulphur, this affluence was obvious in the way that guests arrived. Trains "with sleeping palaces attached" had been stopping at the spring since 1871, but the 1890's saw the start of a boom in private railroad cars. Railroad presidents began it all, for how else would one arrive at White Sulphur but in "private varnish"? It might be Scott of the Pennsylvania, Reinhart of the Santa Fe, King of the Erie, Warfield or Walters of the Atlantic Coast Line. They were soon imitated by those made rich by railroad-generated prosperity.

One car might belong to William K. Vanderbilt (he owned two), another to J. Ogden Armour, a third to Philip Armour. Others might carry Astors, Goelets and Harknesses, Dukes, Drexels, Cadawaladers and Biddles. For this southern watering spot had become a national society resort.

Though the Civil War was seldom mentioned, the confrontation between South and North was not always happy. There was, for example, the afternoon that the young Mrs. Anna Washington Tucker was introduced to a group of newcomers. After a few pleasantries, the conversation turned,

not to the time-hallowed southern topic of who one's parents were, but to the newer question of what they did.

One father, it seemed, was president of a steel company, and another headed a meatpacking empire. A third was a New York investment banker; still another, chairman of a mining concern.

"And your father?" Mrs. Tucker was asked.

"Why he's a farmer," she replied.

There was a short moment of silence and someone quickly changed the subject. But just as soon as Mrs. Tucker departed, the others set to with a vengeance.

"A farmer's girl at The Old White!"

"What is this place coming to?"

"A daughter of the soil!"

This was too much for the woman who had performed the introductions. "I do not believe," said she, "that Mrs. Tucker told you the name of her farm."

"No," yawned the girl from Pittsburgh, "she did not."

"Mount Vernon," the lady replied.

Money, not tradition, made it a heady era. The card game favors were no longer the simple things, now they were silver $30 repoussé hand mirrors or candy dishes, vermeil punch ladles or a set of cut-glass perfume bottles. Soon the private railroad car was not status symbol enough, now one had to bring a baggage car of furnishings along as well.

The champagne suppers and fancy dress balls became ever more elaborate. Small wonder, for the newspapers devoted column after column to reporting every extravagant detail.

But changes were in the wind. In 1912 West Virginia voted state-wide prohibition by a better than two to one margin. It thus became the ninth state

---

This color photograph of a "horseless carriage" that was parked near the Baltimore Cottage Row dates from about 1915—far too soon for the lady's skirt to have risen much above the ankle.

to bar sale of alcoholic beverages—seven years in advance of the constitutional amendment that brought national prohibition.

Another amendment would eventually bring an even greater change in the spring-going way of life. And, odd to relate, it was first proposed by a White Sulphur visitor, the Republican president whose family name typifies conservatism. For on June 6, 1910, William Howard Taft asked Congress for a constitutional amendment to legalize the collection of an income tax.

It seemed to be a joking matter. Humorist George Fitch wrote of "an exclusive circle, this income tax class—one which the ordinary wage-earning man cannot hope to enter." Someone suggested that a limit of ten per cent be imposed, but this was laughed down as ridiculous; the tax couldn't ever go half that high. The U.S. Senate, often called the world's most deliberative body, deliberated for less than a day, passing it unanimously. Today's inheritance tax structure originated in 1916—bringing more changes.

The Chesapeake & Ohio was distinctly optimistic about its purchase of White Sulphur Springs, for the changes that taxes would bring to life at the springs had not yet become apparent. In the first place, the price—three annual installments of $50,000—hardly mattered to a concern whose net income was already approaching ten million dollars a year. And with guests who seemed dedicated to outdoing one another in spending money, it was logical to invest in improvements that would attract more such passenger traffic. Unfortunately, the property needed something more than face lifting. The Old White's wooden walls could certainly use several coats of paint; the splintered

boards in its verandah needed replacement; the rooms that had been rented to the public even though their wallpaper was hanging loose in strips should be thoroughly renovated. But it was obvious that all this was just stop-gap. Major changes would have to be made.

Architects were called in at once. To Philadelphia's Harris & Richard partnership was assigned the design of a mineral bath building to replace the rickety wooden shack below the spring. More importantly, the noted New York architect Frederick Junius Sterner was asked to draw plans for a new hotel. He proposed a seven-story, 250-room structure in Georgian style—the building that is the nucleus of today's hotel. Construction took just over three years, and The Greenbrier was ready for guests by September 1913. The public rooms were large enough that all the late-season guests at The Old White were invited to join the press at a banquet and open house. One such guest termed The Greenbrier a "new and gorgeous hostelry which to my mind was like a fairy palace set amid the lights and shadows of the Allegheny hills."

Other improvements were made. A nine-hole golf course, The Lakeside, was opened in 1910, and four years later, the eighteen-hole Old White course. The structure that forms the center of today's Golf and Tennis Club was erected. Tennis courts were put in, and some new cottages built. By the end of June, 1915, the C&O had supplemented its original $150,000 investment with $2,400,000 worth of improvements.

For several years The Greenbrier and The Old White were operated independently, allowing visitors the choice between tradition and more modern comforts. The Greenbrier was open the year round, the older hotel only in summer. But as World War

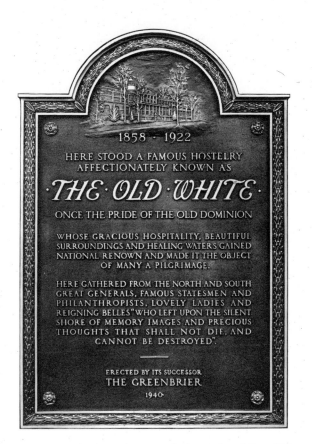

1858 - 1922

HERE STOOD A FAMOUS HOSTELRY
AFFECTIONATELY KNOWN AS

·THE·OLD·WHITE·

ONCE THE PRIDE OF THE OLD DOMINION

WHOSE GRACIOUS HOSPITALITY, BEAUTIFUL
SURROUNDINGS AND HEALING WATERS GAINED
NATIONAL RENOWN AND MADE IT THE OBJECT
OF MANY A PILGRIMAGE.

HERE GATHERED FROM THE NORTH AND SOUTH
GREAT GENERALS, FAMOUS STATESMEN AND
PHILANTHROPISTS, LOVELY LADIES AND
REIGNING BELLES "WHO LEFT UPON THE SILENT
SHORE OF MEMORY IMAGES AND PRECIOUS
THOUGHTS THAT SHALL NOT DIE, AND
CANNOT BE DESTROYED".

ERECTED BY ITS SUCCESSOR
THE GREENBRIER
1940

I came and went, it was obvious that The Old White was running a poor second. In 1922, it failed to pass a state fire inspection, and the order was given to dismantle the historic structure.

Today, a commemorative bronze plaque stands at what was the northwest corner of the old hotel.

It was said that if The Old White's walls could talk, what a story they could tell. Though the walls are no more, much of the old woodwork was preserved. The massive doors of today's Old White Club are among such mementos.

But if The Old White could boast of its famous visitors, The Greenbrier was beginning a similar tradition. President Woodrow Wilson visited the hotel in 1916. He brought his second wife, the former Edith Bolling, back to this scene from her girlhood. (At White Sulphur, a youngster had ruined her blue taffeta gown by wiping candy-sticky hands on it.)

There was General of the Armies John J. Pershing who, in the peaceful atmosphere of White Sulphur, completed his two-volume history of World War I. This book won him a Pulitzer Prize.

But perhaps the most noted visitor of the era was Edward Albert Christian George Andrew

Patrick David Windsor, heir to the British throne. The Prince of Wales' 1919 visit to The Greenbrier lasted four days. Though it was billed as a rest stop, the prince set a lively pace for his entourage. On arrival at the White Sulphur railroad station in a private railroad car, he chose to walk to The Greenbrier, an act that probably makes him unique among v.i.p. guests. The hotel was banked with his favorite red roses, but he hardly noticed them. After a few minutes in his suite, he was off to the swimming pool and golf course, with a moment out to taste the White Sulphur water. In the evenings, there was dancing, for the State Department had arranged to have a number of pretty and oh-so-eligible young socialities on hand. The prince demonstrated that he was one of the boys by sitting in for a few moments as drummer with the hotel orchestra.

Sunday found him in White Sulphur Springs' Episcopal Church, and the service, read from an old edition of The Book of Common Prayer, included the phrase "God bless the Prince and Princess of Wales.*"

"I took a bit of ribbing on that," the prince was quoted by Cleveland Amory, "but it's rather more amusing to look back on now, don't you think?"

The woman for whom King Edward VIII would renounce his throne had also been a White Sulphur visitor. In her first vacations at the spring, "Bessiewallis" Warfield stayed in a cottage on Baltimore Row with her family, as did Betsy Patterson, that other Baltimore Row belle who married into European royalty.

Miss Warfield, in addition, spent the first of her three honeymoons at The Greenbrier. She recalled in her memoirs that she was "relaxed and happy at White Sulphur...we both enjoyed the beauty and the comfort of the place."

The income tax amendment began its challenge to affluent spring-goers in the twenties. For though the basic income tax rate of one per cent stayed the same, the surtax on high-bracket incomes that had been set at some 60 per cent during World War I was kept almost as high. Though there was a recession in 1921, much of the decade was prosperous. In 1925, a second eighteen-hole golf course, the Greenbrier, was built at White Sulphur Springs. During the 1929 season, plans

---

* The reference was to that other U.S. visitor, the former King Edward VII and his wife, the Princess Alexandra.

*Two noted visitors to The Greenbrier
in the years following World War I
were General of the Armies John J. Pershing
and the Prince of Wales
who was to become King Edward VIII, and
later, the Duke of Windsor.*

were being readied for an expansion of the hotel itself, for patronage had been steadily increasing.

Did this mean that the spa, unlike the Calwell days of old, was showing a profit? Unfortunately, no. But the Van Sweringen brothers of Cleveland, then the C&O's controlling stockholders, had enough operating income that they really didn't care. They used The Greenbrier to entertain both the owners of railroad properties that they wished to acquire and the major freight shippers on their rail empire, which included the C&O, Erie, Nickel Plate and Pere Marquette railroads, among others. Thus, a hotel that could shrink its losses from $120,000 in 1925 to $70,000 in 1928 was of little financial concern to them.

The same philosophy prevailed in the months that followed the 1929 stock crash. For in 1930 and 1931, at a time when most businesses were retrenching if not already bankrupt, the C&O spent $3,400,000 on its White Sulphur property. Most of that went to expand the main Greenbrier structure from 250 to 580 rooms. A residential wing was built to the north, joining the older hotel to the baths building. On the south, the dining areas were doubled, an auditorium was added, and the Virginia wing erected. All of the cottages were thoroughly renovated, and, where necessary, rebuilt. So The Greenbrier began the thirties in the best of physical shape.

Potential patrons recognized this fact. Many families who had been dividing their time among several residences closed most of them down and spent the summer months at The Greenbrier. What made this easy was that their children could attend classes of the famous Graham-Eckes School, which then wintered in Daytona Beach and maintained summer sessions at White Sulphur.

Enough guests brought chauffeurs that a special clubroom was opened for them, complete with writing desks and pool table.

In 1932, bowing to demand from guests, the hotel set up a polo field, and organized matches began. Within three years, the game was being played so often that a second field was needed. Fencing, indoor archery and golf-driving ranges were set up. The Old White golf course was reconstructed in 1933, and the Greenbrier eighteen was done over the next year.

With Mason and Dixon tournaments in both golf and tennis, play-offs for the Davis Cup tennis team, and the championship polo matches, The Greenbrier was making quite a name for itself with sportsmen. But 1936 also saw a sports event of quite another variety. It began when Alva Bradley, owner of the Cleveland Indians baseball team and member of the C&O board of directors, was hit on the rump by a golf ball being played by a new Greenbrier employee.

"How dare you drive from the fairway into an occupied green?" shouted Bradley at his 23-year-old assailant. The youngster tried to explain, but the director ordered both the golf manager and the hotel's general manager to fire him. He was reprieved only after demonstrating his long-hitting style in a round of golf with Bradley. For Samuel Jackson Snead had not hit the board member with a shot from the fairway, but with a 335-yard drive from the tee.

The Snead saga is one of America's notable success stories. Born in 1912—the same year as Ben Hogan and Byron Nelson—Snead was raised near Hot Springs, Virginia, where his father farmed a small acreage in a valley "so narrow that dogs had

to wag their tails up and down." Sam was introduced to golf by an older brother, and got his early practice with a club made out of a swamp maple limb with a knot on one end. One of his early drives, at age seven, lofted a stone through a church window; he then hid in the woods to avoid discovery. (Thirty years later, he gave the church an electric organ.) After graduating from high school, Snead took jobs behind a soda fountain and as a short order cook, but soon became an assistant in The Homestead's golf shop. After winning the third prize in the 1936 Cascades Open using a makeshift set of clubs, The Greenbrier's golf manager, Fred Martin, offered him the chance to become a professional at White Sulphur Springs —and a career was launched.

Since then, Snead has won well over a hundred tournaments, including three Professional Golfers Association championships, three U.S. Masters, three Canadian Opens, two Western Opens and a British Open title. Though the U.S. Open championship has eluded him, he has been runner-up four times. The 1964 edition of *The Encyclopedia of Golf* ranks him first in the number of tournaments won between 1940 and 1963, as well as leading money winner.

But perhaps the high point of his career came in the 1959 Greenbrier Open, when he carded an eleven-under-par 59, the record in PGA-sanctioned tournament play. Snead presented the ball to The Greenbrier's golf manager, the same Fred Martin who had hired him back in 1936.

For Greenbrier guests in the thirties who preferred less active pleasures than golf, an art colony was established in the cottage rows, with instruction available from painters, sculptors, and other specialists. Touring art and photographic exhibi-

tions were featured. A motion picture club acted out and filmed its own productions.

In a historic sense, the important event of the thirties was the opening of the Presidents' Cottage Museum. A painstaking search was made for old books, letters and manuscripts dealing with White Sulphur. Artifacts used by famous guests were collected to be put on display. The museum was opened in 1932, as part of Robert E. Lee Week, which marked the sixty-fifth anniversary of Lee's 1867 visit. Baltimore "G" cottage received a plaque commemorating his stay there; a memorial tree was planted; the Confederate graves in the cemetery were visited. A grand ball was the final event, and participants drilled themselves in the old dances—the White Sulphur Riley, the Varsouvianna, lancers and reels. And immediately following the grand march, a large portrait of Lee and Traveller was unveiled by Mrs. Woodrow Wilson. The portrait had been painted by Natalie Eynon Grauer, whose not-so-artistic smears had ruined Mrs. Wilson's blue taffeta dress many years before. By now the two women could joke with each other about it.

Among other participants in the Lee Week ceremonies were General Harry Rene Lee and several other family members, the governors of Virginia and South Carolina, Attorney Henry Waters Taft and Dr. Francis Pendleton Gaines, president of Washington and Lee University. Three guests who had met General Lee during his visits to White Sulphur were in attendance, but a fourth didn't make it. Though Miss Christiana Bond, chronicler of Lee's first postwar visit, would live to celebrate her 100th birthday in 1944, she was taken seriously ill a few days before her scheduled visit, and could not attend.

On the 65th anniversary of Robert E. Lee's first visit to White Sulphur Springs, a plaque honoring the cottage he used was dedicated by Mrs. Woodrow Wilson.

Lee Week was so successful that it was continued through the thirties, along with an Old White Week. A special event for the 1940 Old White Week was the premiere of "Greenbrier," an operetta by Emma Gray Trigg and Elizabeth Bull Maury. The plot involved romance and intrigue at The Old White during the Spanish American War. In the key episode, a box of harmless mosquitoes was substituted for one containing yellow fever insects that had been brought to White Sulphur by spies masquerading as dancing instructors. The *Richmond Times-Dispatch* reported that this scene gave hotel management much satisfaction for the man who made the substitution uttered the line:

"I couldn't find no mosquitoes at White Sulphur. I had to go 38 miles, clear over to Hot Springs, to find them."

Well anyway, the singing and dancing were fun. And the Richmond paper provided one example of changing southern customs: It reported that a Metro-Goldwyn-Mayer talent scout was in the audience—the type of news no southern newspaper would have once considered reporting.

The aeroplane was to bring its own changes. The Greenbrier's airport, which had opened in 1929 on the site of the resort's second racetrack, had become a busy refueling stop for the light planes in use at the time.

Amelia Earhart flew in one afternoon during an aimless cross-country flight. Such "vagabonding" was her antidote to "writer's cramp," for she was then an associate editor of *Cosmopolitan* magazine.

Mayor Curley of Boston was a short-term Greenbrier guest during a flight to Georgia; the military made it their usual stop between Washington and Wright Field in Ohio, for it was large enough that full squadrons could land in formation. Some days, sixty or seventy planes were on the field at once.

The airport was more than a stop in transit. Powell Crosley, Jr., often flew friends to White Sulphur in "Lesgo," his Douglas Amphibian. Other business executives commuted by air for weekends with their families. Many guests took short flights. One favorite was a flying tour of Virginia's Civil War battlefields. Another was for picnic lunches. In fact, just before the start of World War II, plans were being made to clear an autogiro landing space atop nearby White Rock Mountain so that Greenbrier guests could picnic there in style.

Then came Pearl Harbor—and shortly thereafter a request from Greenbrier visitor Cordell Hull, now U.S. secretary of state, that the hotel house interned diplomats and foreign newspaper correspondents. The relative isolation of The Greenbrier's location made it easy to guard. On December 21, 1941, the first contingent of 159 Germans and Hungarians arrived by special train. It was a subdued Christmas for the 15 children in the group, though a teutonic Kris Kringle did arrive at a party in the hotel auditorium to distribute gifts.

Meanwhile, when residents of the White Sulphur area discovered that national enemies were being quartered at The Greenbrier, they began to protest. A mass meeting was held in nearby Lewisburg, but officials were able to quell the potential trouble by pointing out that American diplomats and newsmen were in German hands. It was quid pro quo; what happened to the Germans at White Sulphur would affect treatment of Americans at Bad Nauheim, a German mineral spa. The State Department sent the hotel daily reports on menus

k Times Company.

rk Times.

LATE CITY EDITION
Partly cloudy and mild today followed by cloudy and colder in late afternoon or night.

Temperatures Yesterday—Max., 52; Min., 39

ECEMBER 20, 1941.

THREE CENTS NEW YORK CITY and Vicinity

IDANAO, BATTLE RAGES;
HONG KONG, HOLD HILLS;
DRAFT MEN FROM 20 TO 44

ONY IS CUT OFF

Kong's Garrison
sists at Strong
oints on Island

FIGHT TO LAST

Claims Capture of
ictoria—Dock Area
Reported Ablaze

By The United Press.

NDON, Dec. 19—The fate
ong Kong, farthest Imperial
t of Britain's far-flung em-
was apparently sealed tonight
he hard-pressed garrison
a gallant but seemingly
ss fight against Japanese
landed on the main island
Crown Colony.

Colonial Office announced
0 o'clock tonight that a report
Japanese sources that Hong
was in Japanese hands could
e confirmed or denied, since
essage had been received from
colony since early this morn-

Communications of Hong Kong
th Chungking also ceased.
okyo radio reports heard in
nila said Hong Kong had
n in Japanese hands since 11
. yesterday, Tokyo time. A
ei dispatch reported from
n by the Andi Agency of
ntina to The Associated
said the Japanese flag was
over the harbor, and the
British resistance was rap-
being broken. Another
ei report said the Japanese
ed their landing on Hong
Island in small boats after
lve-hour artillery barrage
air bombing had prepared
y. Fortifications opposite
n were reported destroyed
e large Taikoo dock area
flames. The landings
apparently made in this
, with the Japanese quick-
pying Jardine's Lookout,
center

Nazi Diplomats Are Sent
To West Virginia Resort

Dr. Hans Thomsen, chargé d'affaires, and his wife before leaving yesterday for White Sulphur Springs.   Associated Press Wirephoto

Special to THE NEW YORK TIMES.

WASHINGTON, Dec. 19—The German Embassy staff and German newspaper correspondents, numbering about 150, were sent to White Sulphur Springs, W. Va., today pending their departure from the United States when arrangements have been completed. The staff traveled in buses except for Dr. Hans Thomsen, the chargé d'affaires, and his wife, who rode in a limousine. The Swiss Lega-

tion took over custody of the German Embassy.

The Hungarian Legation staff of about twelve is also being concentrated at the West Virginia resort, while Japanese consular staffs from all over the United States are being sent to Hot Springs, Va. The Japanese Embassy is remaining here in the embassy for the present. No announcement

Continued on Page Six

has been made concerning the removal of the Italian Embassy staff.

American diplomats and newspaper correspondents in Germany have been concentrated at Bad Nauheim, a resort in Southern Germany. The staff of the American Embassy in Tokyo is housed in embassy buildings. The State Department, however, was not ready to confirm today a report that the American and Japanese diplomats would be exchanged through the use of an Argentine steamship. Arrangements looking to their repatriation on a reciprocal basis were being made, it was said, but had not been completed.

Contrary to the impression of some enemy aliens that recent Presidential proclamations would not allow them to travel anywhere, Attorney General Biddle announced today that certain latitude would be permitted in this regard.

Pending the issuance of detailed regulations, Mr. Biddle announced that the Presidential proclamations of Dec. 7 and Dec. 8 did not forbid the following:

"Travel within the boundaries or limits of the municipality, town, village, locality or community in which he resides, from place to place and in such manner as will permit him to engage in the activities usual in his community;

"Coming from his home to his place of business, or

"Travel between his home and his place of religious worship, school, college or institution of learning at which he is in regular attendance, or any Federal, State or local government agency with which he is required to transact business."

Whenever an alien enemy wishes to change his address he must first notify the United States Attorney in his district.

Diplomats Installed in Hotel

By The Associated Press.

WHITE SULPHUR SPRINGS, W. Va., Dec. 19—Staffs of the German Embassy and the Hungarian Legation and members of their families arrived here today and were installed at a hotel.

On official of the State Department who declined to be quoted said that other Germans, some from embassies and consulates in South American countries, were expected to join the party here.

Members of the party will have full range of the hotel grounds, golf course and recreation facilities while here for an indefinite stay, pending departure from the United States.

British Bring Foe to a Halt
In Malaya, but Yield Pena

ARTIST GOES TO BELLEVUE

The Greenbrier Independent.

Greenbrier And Cottages Officially Closed; Taken Over By Government

Many Historical Items From Famous Resort Are Preserved

The Greenbrier hotel and cottages in White Sulphur Springs was officially closed to all guests on Monday night and was taken over by the government for an army base hospital on Tuesday.

As the last guests gathered in the spacious and magnificent lobby to depart for the C. & O. station, the hotel organist at the request of General Manager Loren R. Johnston played a closing organ recital, beginning with the beloved old southern tunes, "Carry Me Back to Old Virginia," "My Old Kentucky Home," and many other appropriate songs ending with the stirring patriotic "God Bless America" and the national anthem.

Tears flowed openly and unashamed as guests of many seasons here said their last goodbys to the famous old hotel and the lights blinked out in the upper stories.

The management of the hotel is doing everything possible to preserve its historical items. The Old White museum, which was housed in the Lee cottage, has been turned over to the Greenbrier county library and museum at Lewisburg, which will be closed for the present and a public re-opening will be held at a later date. One set of murals in the President's cottage which depicted life at the Greenbrier have been removed by the artist, Wm. C. Grauer, to be sent to Washington and Lee university at Lexington. Other items such as old prints will also be sent to the university.

The library of the hotel goes to the local Community House. Sam Snead was presented with five scrapbooks, which contained newspaper clippings of his activities as America's number 1 golfer, while at the Greenbrier. This scrapbook is said to contain such clippings as the visit of the Prince of Wales, 1919, and 125 other scrapbooks bearing upon the activities here since the opening of the first Greenbrier—these 125 books will go to the archives of the C. & O. Railroad at Richmond, Virginia. The golf course and swimming pool will remain open to the public for a brief period, pending negotiations. The personnel director of the surgeon general's office has arrived for the purpose of determining from the different department heads, who desires to remain in the service. The staffs of the diningroom, kitchen, and household-keeping departments are leaving for hotels in New York, Williamsburg, Cleveland, etc.

The interest of such a change in so historic a place as White Sulphus Springs, and this Greenbrier Hotel, spreads its wings to the very fringes of civilization, and once again places our "little Mountain State" in an enviable lime-light. To those of us who have even just glimpsed the place it passes before our fancied vision in new Kaleidoscopic colors for memory's casket. It carries us back to 1932, when our "Mount Vernon, Its Children, Its Romances, Its Allied Mansions and Families" had just come from the press in revised form, and brought to us an invitation among the other "Lee Authors" to attend "Lee Week" here. We had hoped

General Dwight D. Eisenhower first visited The Greenbrier during World War II when it was an army hospital. He is shown, at left, with Colonel D. C. Elkin and General Clyde Beck of the hospital's staff, and, right, during a visit with some patients.

and accommodations provided to U.S. diplomats so that things could be kept on a precise parallel.

Soon a Japanese contingent arrived (they had previously been quartered at The Homestead). The total number of internees reached almost 1,400. These persons had been told that when repatriated, they would be allowed to take all their household and personal belongings, but no money. As a result, they descended on The Greenbrier's concession shops to convert their dollars into repatriable items. Soon the stores had been literally stripped to the walls—but then one merchant had a brainstorm. He brought in Sears Roebuck and Montgomery Ward catalogs, and the buying began again.

One of the hotel's musicians bribed a diplomat's child to roam the corridors singing "God Bless America." Guests glared but maintained a diplomatic silence.

During one meal, an internee walked up to the bandstand to ask the name of the selection that had just been played. "The White Cliffs of Dover," it turned out.

By July 15, 1942, the prisoner exchange had been completed, and two weeks later The Greenbrier reopened for civilian business.

But normalcy lasted only a month, for on September 1, the Army took over. Where the State Department, in effect, had leased the hotel, the Army bought it outright for $3 million—leaving the C&O a loss of several million. But, of course, this was war.

As many of the murals, pictures and old engravings as possible were hastily shipped off into storage, loaned to museums and donated to the Washington and Lee University. Furnishings that would not be used in the hospital were auctioned. On August 29 was held a farewell mint julep party; the

resort's guests and friends raised a final toast—"To The Greenbrier."

The hotel was quickly converted. A hospital-style elevator was cut through one corner of the ballroom; operating equipment was installed in sixth-floor rooms, and by November, Ashford General Hospital was ready for business. Specializing in vascular and neurological surgery, it became one of the country's largest hospitals—reaching a peak of 2,720 patients. In addition, over two thousand prisoners of war were sheltered in a camp near the Greenbrier Airport.

But some things stayed the same. In view of the hotel's historic traditions, it was allowed to remain white, not repainted in military colors. The hotel carpets remained on most floors, the crystal chandeliers in place, though the dining room became a cafeteria. The Virginia Room, with its murals of old resort life on the walls, became a recreation room. Unfortunately, the soldiers enjoyed playing darts with the murals. The Presidents' Cottage became headquarters for the Red Cross; the Golf and Tennis Club, an officers' club.

Among those who came to the hospital were Generals Jonathan Wainwright, Brehon Sommervell, Mark Clark and Dwight Eisenhower. One of the few non-military customers was the retired secretary of state, Cordell Hull.

To the wounded who came to White Sulphur from the war fronts, the Allegheny mountains performed their peaceful magic. In the words of one such visitor, it was his "Shangri-La."

And then, peace. When Ashford General Hospital closed its doors on September 5, 1946, the property was declared surplus and offered for sale. The way had now been cleared for The Greenbrier's rebirth.

RETURN TO ELEGANCE

"We doubt that even the Sultan of Turkey,
the Emperor of China or the
Czar of Russia... ever attempted
anything more colossal."

A man with a dream—Robert R. Young—and a woman in a wheelchair—Dorothy Draper.

These, in sum, were the personalities that started The Greenbrier on its return to elegance. Their intervention was fortunate, since in those uncertain early postwar days, it was doubtful that the Chesapeake & Ohio would repurchase the White Sulphur hotel. There were some within the railway system who felt that the C&O was well rid of the property, since no one knew where the postwar years would lead their railroad—or any other railroad, for that matter. They argued that it would be unwise to make the major investment needed to rehabilitate The Greenbrier; the situation differed from pre-war years, when the railway was involved with an already operating property. The chances for repurchase seemed so dim that the mayor of White Sulphur Springs attempted to organize a local company to buy the property and turn it over to the railroad for operation.

Then came the man with a dream. Actually, Robert R. Young was a man with many dreams, and as with any such visionary, it is difficult to say exactly why he decided to repurchase the White Sulphur property. No doubt it was part of his plan to encourage passenger traffic on the C&O. And this, in turn, was certainly a part of his vision of a transcontinental railroad system based on the C&O —an idea that had intrigued the Van Sweringens before him, and Collis P. Huntington a few steps further back. But it may have been more simple than all that; perhaps Young did it because someone told him it couldn't be done.

The Cameo Ballroom's new nine-foot-wide chandelier is a high spot of The Greenbrier's redecoration following its use as a World War II military hospital. The hotel was reopened in 1948.

Ever since Young became the C&O's controlling stockholder in the mid-thirties, he had been sparring with "old guard" New York bankers and with more traditional railroad men in other systems. While much of his success was due to skill in the stock market, Young was one of the first financiers to cultivate the small stockholder—a revolutionary gambit at the time. One of his methods was to cultivate passenger traffic. Young became a pioneer advocate of rail credit cards, instant reservation systems, dome-view cars, and hostesses and motion pictures on trains. Most of Young's ideas have been tried by various other railroads in the years since he first proposed them, but the ideas were his. Thus, where others might have encouraged passenger traffic merely by purchasing a hotel, Young specified that it should be one of the finest hotels anywhere. And the $3,300,000 he paid the government for the buildings and 6,500 acres of land was only a starter.

Here the woman in a wheelchair, Dorothy Draper, enters the story. The former Dorothy Tuckerman, a socialite from Tuxedo Park, made her first inspection of the Greenbrier property by wheelchair—while her broken ankle was in a cast. Since there was no electric power at the time, the inspection was by flashlight. Perhaps it was this lack of lights, perhaps the original design, but she felt the place was a brobdingnagian monster of a bowling alley, for there was a 20-foot-high passage from the Terrace Dining Room at one end of the building straight through to the Presidents' Parlor at the other end—a distance of over a fifth of a mile. Such a length would tend to dwarf anyone who walked through the main lobby, and so she planned to add walls that would minimize the total length of the building without cutting the public

President Dwight D. Eisenhower
is welcomed to The Greenbrier
by the late Walter Tuohy (right).
Looking on are Cyrus Eaton, C&O Chairman,
and, at left, Truman Wright,
Greenbrier Vice President.

spaces up into pieces so tiny that people would feel cramped. In place of one doorway, she put a wood-burning fireplace, and over it hung a Jane Stuart portrait of George Washington. Other walls were built, and arches strategically placed to provide ever-changing vistas as one walks from one lobby area to another.

Equally as important in Mrs. Draper's basic plan was the decision to separate the "public room" and registration functions of the lobby, for in pre-war days, both had taken place on the same lobby floor. Thus, the front entrance's porte cochère was extended and a stairway cut through to the hotel's lower floor. Both the upper public rooms and the lower lobby were tied together through the use of an identical checkerboard pattern of black and white marble—but with guest check-ins and baggage handled in the lower areas, the upper spaces remained uncluttered. Irene Corbally Kuhn, writing in *Town and Country*, remarked that "1,250 guests seem no more than a good-sized gay country house party."

Where historic furnishings of the old hotel were still in place, or could be rescued from storage, they were again put to use. The list of such items includes the Sheffield chandelier and the Queen Anne table in the Presidents' Parlor, the antique girandole mirror in the Victorian writing room, five Czechoslovakian chandeliers in the Colonnades dining room. To these were added such new gems as the custom-made nine-foot chandelier in the Cameo Ballroom and a $5,000 Aubusson rug purchased for the Presidents' Parlor. (This rug had to be retired some years later when women began wearing spike-heeled shoes.)

For sleeping-floor corridors, Mrs. Draper designed a rhododendron-patterned wallpaper that saluted West Virginia's state flower; for individual rooms, she created a range of fabric, paint and wallpaper choices that allowed no two of the 580 rooms to be exactly alike in decoration. Moreover, rooms on lower floors that overlooked a garden vista were done in solid colors; those on upper levels used printed fabrics or wallpapers. Rooms facing east utilized a warm color scheme, while those on the west were given cooler colors.

The color contrasts she used could have gone awfully wrong in less talented hands. Bright green chairs might be placed in a room with light blue walls, and the total effect livened up with a few touches of red. The ideas executed by her Greenbrier staff added up to a concept in decorating that has since been echoed in many other hotels.

During most of The Greenbrier reconstruction and redecoration, things went as scheduled, but there were some problems. The entire carved-plaster ceiling of the Cameo Ballroom, for example, collapsed and had to be redone from scratch.

As 1948 began, preparation started for a grand opening party on April 15–18. And though a few things still had to be completed at the time of a preview for some C&O customers, everything but the swimming pool was in readiness for the opening celebration itself, an event that *Life* magazine termed the "most lavish" such party of the century.

In 14 private railroad cars (shades of the good old days!), by limousine and by private plane arrived such luminaries as the Duke and Duchess of Windsor, Prince and Princess Alexander Hohenlohe, the Marchioness of Hartington (Kathleen Kennedy), Lady Stanley, Lady Cochran, Lady Harry Oakes and Lady Sheila Milbank; the *Social Register*'s Winthrop Aldrich, Mr. and Mrs. John

The 1956 North American Summit Conference saw President Adolfo Cortines of Mexico, President Eisenhower, and Prime Minister Louis St. Laurent of Canada make a public appearance on The Greenbrier's front lawn.

Jacob Astor, Mr. and Mrs. Anthony Biddle Duke, Mrs. Nicholas du Pont, Mrs. Harrison Williams, Mr. and Mrs. Winston Guest, and many, many others.

After scanning the guest list, one Registerite remarked: "Anybody who shows up at The Colony this weekend is a social outcast."

From the world of politics came Senators Charles Tobey, Scott Lucas and Burton K. Wheeler, Attorney General Tom Clark, West Virginia Governor and Mrs. Clarence W. Meadows, Virginia Governor and Mrs. William Tuck, and New Jersey Governor and Mrs. Charles Edison. Among those present was young Representative John Fitzgerald Kennedy. His parents had honeymooned at White Sulphur in 1915, and his mother and several of his sisters were at the house party.

Others on the guest list included Perle Mesta, Elsa Maxwell, William Randolph Hearst, Jr., J. Arthur Rank and Bing Crosby. (Crosby claimed that the maid who cleaned his room used a mink mop, and checked for dust with a lorgnette.)

With dancing on Thursday, Friday and Saturday evenings, a garden party, cocktail parties, ladies' golf and a men's pro-amateur tournament, the time was well filled. Aptly enough, the movies screened were "Mr. Blandings Builds His Dream House" and "The Emperor Waltz." As a climax came the Saturday evening Diamond Ball. In almost conscious imitation of White Sulphur's older era, there were silver mirrors as favors for the ladies—but Scandinavian modern, not repoussé. A $2,000 diamond cigarette case was auctioned off for charity. Meyer Davis, his orchestra and virtuoso drummer (a Duke who presented an encore to a 1919 performance in the same setting) played "How Are Things in Glocca Morra?"

Though no one invoked the specter of the Sun King, Elsa Maxwell was sure that the party "outshone the dreams of a Haroun-al-Raschid." Raved Cholly Knickerbocker: "We doubt that even the Sultan of Turkey, the Emperor of China or the Czar of Russia, when these fabulous courts were at their peak, ever attempted anything on a more colossal scale." (He thus proved himself one who didn't hold a grudge, for at the party's start, his ex-wife had been ushered to the suite he and his current wife were to occupy.)

One socialite remarked there had been "nothing like it since the Bradley Martin ball in 1896." And even Cleveland Amory—a reporter seldom given to promiscuous hyperbole—called it "the outstanding resort society function in modern social history."

For its encore, The Greenbrier transformed this opening party into an annual Spring Festival. On their visits to it, the Duke and Duchess of Windsor always made a point of competing in the Viennese waltz contest, a feature of the festival's champagne Anniversary Ball. (The Windsors' residence while at The Greenbrier was the Presidential Suite, a virtual mansion within the hotel's Virginia Wing. This duplex suite includes a living room, study, library, office, dining room and service kitchen, and—upstairs—seven bedrooms, a sitting room, and seven baths.)

*T*he Presidential Suite was first put to its named use—by a president of the United States—on March 25, 1956, when Dwight D. Eisenhower held his North American Summit Conference with President Adolfo Cortines of Mexico and Prime Minister Louis St. Laurent of Canada at White Sulphur Springs.

65

It was almost unprecedented in diplomatic annals. "The president," wrote the *New York Times'* James Reston, "has made a point of having no agenda, of 'creating a good atmosphere' and of avoiding any rigid rules of negotiation and protocol." Rather than house only the United States delegation in the Presidential Suite, Eisenhower insisted that the three heads of government stay there, with lesser members of each party elsewhere in the hotel. The Greenbrier easily took care of the aides and bodyguards as well as 138 accredited newsmen and photographers, without neglecting its other guests. Some guests, however, were a bit surprised when the Signal Corps' switchboard operators answered, "Greenbrier White House."

As the conference ended, Eisenhower said to St. Laurent, "Let's do it again, and here." Unfortunately, shifting political fortunes soon pulled St. Laurent out of office, and the conference was not repeated. Eisenhower's successor, John F. Kennedy, had considered entertaining France's Charles de Gaulle at The Greenbrier during his projected 1964 state visit, but this plan was cut short by Kennedy's tragic death late in 1963. President Lyndon B. Johnson* first visited White Sulphur while vice president.

* Though early records are incomplete, President Johnson's visit apparently made him the 18th president to visit White Sulphur. Others were Andrew Jackson, Martin Van Buren, John Tyler, Zachary Taylor, Millard Fillmore, Franklin Pierce, James K. Polk, James Buchanan, Ulysses S. Grant, Rutherford B. Hayes, Chester A. Arthur, Benjamin Harrison, William McKinley, William Howard Taft, Woodrow Wilson, Dwight D. Eisenhower, and John F. Kennedy. In addition, a number of presidents' wives are on the rolls: Mrs. Grover Cleveland, Mrs. Calvin Coolidge, Mrs. Herbert Hoover and Mrs. Franklin D. Roosevelt.

The hotel's appeal to visiting dignitaries can perhaps be summed up in two comments. Jawaharlal Nehru, the late prime minister of India, wrote in The Greenbrier's guest book:

"Two nights and a day is far too brief a period to stay in this very fine hotel situated in lovely surroundings. Yet even that is worthwhile, and we have thoroughly enjoyed our stay here. We shall remember Greenbrier."

President Eisenhower, following his 1956 summit meeting, wrote Truman Wright, Greenbrier Vice President, as follows:

"I can't leave The Greenbrier without once again expressing to you, and through you to the members of your staff, my sincere appreciation of the courteous and efficient helpfulness that we have found on every side. I know only too well that the intrusion of a party such as ours, complicated by the separate arrivals of the President of Mexico and the Prime Minister of Canada and the members of their staffs, means disruption and confusion even to such a well-run and large establishment as you have here. The fact that you have absorbed all of us so easily is a tribute to you and your associates."

This ability to absorb many people with ease is a valuable Greenbrier attribute, for in the hotel economics of today, few establishments of over 100 rooms can exist without business meetings and conferences. As one of the nation's larger hotels, the 650-room Greenbrier is certainly no exception —but unlike many less fortunate ones, its size and physical design are such that these groups meet in areas some distance away from the hotel's main public areas.

"But," says Manager Wesler Keenan, "we still actively court the individual guest; we value and need his patronage."

Among the notable visitors to The Greenbrier since its reopening in 1948 have been Jawaharlal Nehru and his sister, Madame Pandit, Prince Ranier and Princess Grace of Monaco with their family, and Presidents John F. Kennedy and Lyndon B. Johnson.

For its winter weekends, The Greenbrier has found a major group customer in the Chesapeake & Ohio's own shareowners. In 1959, with encouragement from Robert Young's successor as C & O Board Chariman, Cyrus Eaton, and President Walter J. Tuohy, the first of many winter-rate stockholder house parties was scheduled. Since then, more than 15,000 stockholders have attended such gatherings, and the weekends sell out almost as soon as announced. *Forbes* magazine termed the concept "one of those rare ideas that builds good will for a company and makes money for it at the same time." In each year since 1959, The Greenbrier has paid its parent C&O a substantial dividend.

Maintenance of this close relationship with stockholders is obviously important to the C&O's new president, Gregory S. DeVine, who was elected to the post in 1964 when Mr. Tuohy became C&O vice-chairman and chief executive officer of both the C&O and its recent affiliate, the Baltimore & Ohio Railroad.

Another tie between railroad and hotel is the Greenbrier Clinic, established in 1948. The idea of a diagnostic clinic in a resort setting originated with Robert Young and former Secretary of State Edward R. Stettinius, and was developed in conjunction with the C&O's medical and surgical staff. Stettinius, who was one of the original planners of the United Nations, had seen many executives in business and government become disabled by diseases that, in most cases, could have been cured if caught in time. He believed that most such executives put off medical examinations because they were repelled by the atmosphere of a hospital. (After all, such institutions are set up primarily to treat those who are already sick.) So the Greenbrier Clinic opened its doors specifically to provide examinations for the healthy.

Dr. James P. Baker, medical director of the clinic since its inception, points out that back in 1948 "we didn't know if this idea of preventive medicine would catch on. Before then, all clinics were designed for sick people or people with medical complaints of some kind. Our clinic was then unique in that it was designed exclusively for diagnosis, not treatment."

Working with Dr. Baker are associate physicians who specialize in internal medicine. An advisory panel of 16 distinguished specialists under the chairmanship of Dr. Chester Keefer is available to staff physicians for consultation.

Each year, approximately 2,500 persons, one third of them women, go through the clinic's three-day series of tests and examinations. By design, these activities occupy only the mornings, and enrollees are encouraged to spend the afternoons on golf course, tennis court and riding trail —or if they choose, just doing nothing. (The *Wall Street Journal's* quip that tests are coordinated with golf starting times thus actually reverses the cause and effect.)

Today, almost a hundred major business concerns send top executives (who, in some cases, bring their wives) for checkups. Even when a corporation pays a man's bill, the diagnosis is discussed only with the patient himself or his personal physician.

In White Sulphur's early years, many of those who came to consult Dr. Moorman and have him prescribe the spring waters were repeat visitors to the spa. Today, many clinic visitors are also repeaters, for annual examinations are encouraged. When a Greenbrier Clinic diagnostician has conducted,

This famous foursome waits its turn at the Old White Golf Course tee—former C&O Chairman Robert R. Young, with Christopher Dunphy, the Duke of Windsor and Charles Cushing.

say, six such check-ups on an individual, he knows a patient's medical history with ever-increasing precision. Thus a diagnostician's warning to "slow down" or change working habits can be made with greater assurance. When a diet is needed, it can be spelled out. If the diagnosis shows a need for physiotherapy, the patient may choose to try out the treatment in the fully equipped Greenbrier Mineral Bath Department.

Though some types of physiotherapy require a doctor's prescription, the mineral bath that is the department's namesake does not. And the relaxant effect of a hot sulphur water bath is spectacular. On first encounter, the water does have that traditional odor of a "half-boiled, half-spoiled egg." But as one relaxes in a tub of it, everything becomes quite pleasant. After a session, one travel writer remarked, "I felt that I just might buy the whole hotel, possibly the whole of Greenbrier County. My wife allowed as how she'd buy it if I didn't."

Today, no claims of medical cures are made for the sulphur water, but one can easily imagine how Mrs. Anderson could have found relief for her rheumatism back in 1778.

The Bath Department was refurbished in 1962, when the Greenbrier Clinic (which had been located in the mineral bath wing) moved to quarters in the hotel's new West Virginia Wing.

Since The Greenbrier's 1948 reopening, there has been a steady broadening of facilities for sports. In 1953, the Greenbrier Gun Club was built, replacing some older skeet and trap facilities. Four years later, a new Kate's Mountain Lodge and an outdoor swimming pool came into being; soon thereafter came bowling with eight automated lanes. In 1962, the nine-hole Lakeside golf course, first of the three built by the resort, was expanded to

eighteen holes. At the same time, the eighteen-hole Greenbrier course was redesigned to become more challenging. All three of the resort's courses still start and finish at the Golf and Tennis Club—a far cry from White Sulphur's original nine holes on the Montague farm. If one of the original five golfers from 1884 were to arrive on the scene today with his gutta percha balls and home made clubs, he would, no doubt, be astonished.

To those who want to view the scenery, the Greenbrier stables provide a pair of high-stepping bays to pull an old-fashioned buckboard. Saddle horses are available for guests who want to follow the hoofprints of General Lee's Traveller along 200 miles of trails on the nearby mountains. Almost 40 miles of walking trails are also maintained.

Equal in fame to Greenbrier sport is Greenbrier food, for the active life encourages guests to bring large appetites to the table. And it is quite a table.

As part of a gastronomic tradition dating back at least a hundred years, The Greenbrier's staff of fifty chefs is directed by a European traditionalist, Swiss-born Hermann G. Rusch.

Some persons judge the quality of a hotel or restaurant kitchen by its vol-au-vent, say, or its boula boula or sweet-breads financière. But no elaborate production will be quite correct if short cuts have been taken; a classic cuisine demands attention to every step of kitchen procedure. Thus, the best single dish on which to judge a kitchen is a basic one—consommé. And in an era when many restaurants and hotels have turned to soup bases, concentrates and powders, The Greenbrier's consommé still begins with 24 pounds of veal bones and three whole turkeys. It is delicious.

Hugh Lofting, in one of his Doctor Doolittle books, divided the world into two groups, plain

The golfing world's Samuel Jackson Snead joins Senator John D. Hoblitzell, Jr., Vice President Richard M. Nixon and The Greenbrier's Truman Wright for a friendly tour of eighteen holes.

feeders and pickle eaters. The Greenbrier's menus are designed to appeal to both, for even when a thousand dinners must be served, there will be items on the menu that will not appeal to more than a handful of guests—tripes à la mode de Caen, for example. But though The Greenbrier's gastronomic reputation may depend on six orders of tripe or tortue de veau, "the six hundred people who order the shrimp cocktail and the filet mignon must be equally satisfied," Rusch emphasizes.

Also indicative of The Greenbrier's fine cuisine is its culinary training program, established in 1957. Though some other programs have since been set up with federal funds, the private-enterprise White Sulphur course was the first of its type in the nation.

At capacity, The Greenbrier can play host to 1,100 guests. And perhaps the highest tribute that can be paid to Vice President Wright and Manager Keenan is that even with so great a load, their small city of 1,100 employees is unobtrusive.

In an age when many businesses seem to be racing one another in being first to convert to self-service and vending-machine techniques, The Greenbrier chooses to remain constant to its heritage of fine service. For many employees, working at The Greenbrier carries on a tradition of genuinely proud service begun by a father or mother—and in some cases, a generation or two further back. Even for those entirely new to the staff, this pride in good service soon becomes its own way of life.

Following a recent visit, E. B. Weiss, *Advertising Age's* hard-to-please marketing columnist, made this comment:

"I have major retailers tell me time and again that it is impossible to achieve high service stand-

ards in this day and age. I have never agreed—and certainly your achievement substantiates my position. I simply can't tell you how much Mrs. Weiss and I enjoyed our three-day stay."

The late New York columnist Ward Morehouse put it this way: "I consider myself a connoisseur of hotels, having been a hotel guest in all of America's fifty states, in all of the countries of South America, and in cities scattered across the world. I like hotel life, its comfort and conveniences... And now, in 1965, I've come upon a hotel whose splendor outshines them all, The Greenbrier—the luxurious establishment at White Sulphur Springs... The Greenbrier, with its more than 600 rooms, is spotless and faultless, quite the most immaculate hotel in my experience... Bellmen are polite and expert; so are the doormen and telephone girls. Everybody speaks so softly The Greenbrier often seems to be a house of whispers. It's nothing like the tumult of New York."

Indeed, The Greenbrier is what a guest wants to make of it. It can be the quiet serenity of the mountains, the high level of cuisine or of sports facilities, it can be such extra touches as the string trio that plays for afternoon tea in the lobby.

Many years ago, a Greenbrier general manager stated the opinion that disregard for tradition has caused the decline of many famous resorts. "Every large property," he continued, "must maintain certain ideals, for resorts are like people—their character and personality make them stand out from the multitude."

So it was and so it will be, for The Greenbrier remains acutely conscious of its two-century heritage. Indeed, "the sweet views around us" are carefully cherished, and the style and traditions of service remain those of old.

The Greenbrier sits for a formal portrait
in its snug Appalachian valley.
Arriving by train, via the Chesapeake & Ohio
Railway main line
by major highway, and at The White Sulphur Springs
airport (top left), over seventy thousand
guests visit the resort each year.
The main hotel is flanked on the right
by mineral bath and garage buildings,
and on the left by its Virginia Wing.
The high-rising West Virginia Wing, seen
at center left, is connected to the main hotel
by a lower level corridor. This building,
in addition to guest rooms, also houses
The Greenbrier Clinic and an exhibit hall.
Glimpsed through the trees at upper right is
the resort's sports center, Golf and Tennis Club.

Sylvan setting and riding ring
provide a memorable frame
for the Georgian portico of The Greenbrier's
north entrance, which faces the site
where stood White Sulphur Springs'
original hotel, the famous Old White.
Within this portico, the upper and lower
lobbies of the hotel. The main public room
within the hotel proper, the central lobby,
features this painting of a colonial gentleman
by Gilbert Stuart (as well as the portrait
by his daughter of George Washington).
The nearby Colonnades Dining Room
is lighted by five elegant Czechoslovakian
chandeliers that were a feature of
The Greenbrier when it opened in 1913.

For guest groups that desire
their own hotel-within-a-hotel,
several accommodations are available
in the cottages that dot the grounds or
within The Greenbrier itself.
The photo at lower right shows
the parlor of the 4-bedroom State Suite.

For those who prefer creative
pleasures, professional instruction
is available from members
of The Greenbrier's Arts Colony,
located in the historic Alabama Row
cottages shown at top left.
Painting, sculpture, weaving, batik,
pottery, and rug hooking are among the
skills represented in the Colony.

To many of its guests, The Greenbrier's
major attraction is its extensive
sports program, highlighted by three
eighteen-hole golf courses that
begin and end at the Golf and Tennis Club.
Among other sports available to guests
are skeet and trap, at a range
high up on Kate's Mountain (lower left)
and tennis, swimming, archery, horseshoes,
riding and hiking.

CHERISHED TRADITIONS
IN A WORLD OF CHANGE

Stand at The Greenbrier's north portico in the softness
of a summer's night and the past merges into the present,
for once again, the ghosts of history come alive.
And the words of one who drank from the White Sulphur
Spring in 1838 seem just as apt today:

> "From every clime—from far and near—
> They come to pay their homage here.
> Old age, he comes—his gladden'd eye
> Anew with lustre sparkles high;
> And while he quaffs, his heart again
> Goes back to youth—forgets its pain.
> And beauty comes, with face so bright!
> She drinks, and smiles with new delight.
> And cheeks that have grown brown with care,
> The pearly spring makes wondrous fair."

ACKNOWLEDGEMENTS

This history of The Greenbrier and White Sulphur Springs has been based not only on the many printed sources listed in the bibliography but on the recollections and researches of many persons—notably those of Lyle Bryce, The Greenbrier's resident naturalist. A further debt is due to Mrs. Marie Handerson, who was the hotel's social director for many years; and the remarkable collection of early books and other memorabilia maintained in the Presidents' Cottage Museum; to Dr. James P. Baker, medical director of the Greenbrier Clinic; to Kenneth Gillespie, Greenbrier florist and former mayor of White Sulphur Springs; and to Mrs. Margot Coley, The Greenbrier's former publicity director, whose historical files contained, among other items, copies of letters by Robert E. Lee unknown to Lee's biographer, Douglas Southall Freeman, that might have caused him to modify some comments on the postwar Lee. And of course, no book such as this could have been completed without the enthusiasm of Greenbrier Vice President Truman Wright and Manager Wesler Keenan.

Away from The Greenbrier, the author's thanks are due to Perceval Reniers' *Springs of Virginia* which tells its tale so well; Mrs. James Muse Richardson of Roanoke, who graciously made available the memoir of life at White Sulphur written by Dr. John J. Moorman; to Dr. James Hupp and the West Virginia State Department of History and Archives; to the Lewisburg Library and Museum; to the always genial reference staff at the New York Public Library; to the Appomattox Court House National Historical Park staff; as well as to the Library of Congress, the Maryland Historical Society, the Enoch Pratt Library's Maryland Room, the Roanoke Library's Virginia Room, and the Eleutherian Mills Historical Library. A special note of thanks must go to Karl F. Klingelhoeffer Jr., and James C. Robertson of Arndt, Preston, Chapin, Lamb & Keen, who produced the book.

ILLUSTRATION CREDITS

Except where noted, all illustrations have come from The Greenbrier's photograph files, or from the Presidents' Cottage Museum on the hotel grounds. Page 8, Academy of Natural Sciences, Philadelphia; 9, Free Library of Philadelphia; 10, Greenbrier County; 12–13, courtesy Ashton Woodman Reniers; 18, portrait from New York Public Library Picture Collection; 22, Bruce Knight, Pagano; 25, Salem, Va., National Bank; 26, Matthew Brady, New York Public Library Picture Collection; 30, Matthew Brady, Handy Collection, Library of Congress; 31, upper, Maryland Historical Society, lower, George B. McClellan Collection, Library of Congress; 32, Valentine Museum, Richmond; 34, left, Library of Congress, right, Historical Society of Delaware; 35, portrait, National Park Service, houses, Library of Congress; 36, Washington and Lee University; 40, New York Public Library; 41, left, Library of Congress, right, courtesy Mrs. C. Ellis Ellicott; 44, The Gibson Book; 50, drawing, The Gibson Book; 56, right, New York Public Library Picture Collection; 57, Reproduced by permission; © Time Inc. 1954; 61, right, courtesy Roy Sibold; 75, Golf Magazine.

BIBLIOGRAPHY

Adams, Frank Dawson, *The Birth and Development of the Geological Sciences.* New York, 1954.

Alexander, E.P., *Military Memoirs of a Confederate.* New York, 1907.

Allen, Frederick Lewis, *Only Yesterday.* New York, 1931.

Amory, Cleveland, *The Last Resorts.* New York, 1952.

Andrews, Avery De Lano, *My Friend and Classmate, John J. Pershing.* Harrisburg, 1939.

Appletons' Handbook of American Travel, Southern Tour. New York, 1873.

Arese, Francesco, *A Trip to the Prairies and in the Interior of North America, 1837–38.* New York, 1934.

A Trip to the Virginia Springs, or Belles and Beaux of 1835, by a Lady. Lexington, Va., 1843.

Banco, or the Tenant of the Spring. Philadelphia, 1839.

Bassett, John Spencer, *The Life of Andrew Jackson.* New York, 1916.

Basso, Hamilton, *Beauregard, the Great Creole.* New York, 1933.

Baudisch, Oskar, *Magic and Science of Natural Healing Waters.* Saratoga Springs, 1940.

Bayard, Ferdinand, *Voyage dans l'intérieur des États-Unis.* Paris, 1797.

Beiser, Arthur, *The Earth.* New York, 1961.

Bell, John, *Mineral and Thermal Springs of the United States and Canada.* Philadelphia, 1855.

Beyer, Edward, *Album of Virginia.* Richmond, 1858.

Bishop, Joseph B., *Charles Joseph Bonaparte: His Life and Public Service.* New York, 1922.

Bond, Christiana, *Memories of General Robert E. Lee.* Baltimore, 1926.

Bostock, John, and Riley, H.T., *The Natural History of Pliny.* London, 1900.

Burke, William, *The Mineral Springs of Western Virginia.* New York, 1842.

Chesapeake and Ohio Railway Company, *Annual Reports to the Interstate Commerce Commission.* 1910 to the present.

Colvin, D. Leigh, *Prohibition in the United States.* New York, 1926.

Conley, Phil, editor, *West Virginia Encyclopedia.* Charleston, 1929.

Cowan, Robert, *Guide to the Virginia Springs.* Philadelphia, 1851.

Craven, Avery, *Edmund Ruffin, Southerner.* New York, 1932.

Crook, James K., *The Mineral Waters of the United States and Their Therapeutic Uses.* New York, 1899.

Davidson, Marshall B., *Life in America.* Boston, 1951.

Dictionary of American Biography. New York, 1928–1937.

Dies, E. J., *Titans of the Soil.* Chapel Hill, 1924.

Dowd, Clement, *Life of Zebulon B. Vance.* Charlotte, 1897.

Downey, Fairfax, *Portrait of an Era as Drawn by C. D. Gibson.* New York, 1936.

Du Pont, Henry Algernon, *The Campaign of 1864 in the Valley of Virginia and the Expedition to Lynchburg.* New York, 1925.

Eardley, A. J., *Structural Geology of North America.* New York, 1962.

Early, Jubal, *Autobiographical Sketch and Narrative of the War Between the States.* Philadelphia, 1912.

Early, Jubal, *A Memoir of the Last Year of the War for Independence in the Confederate States of America.* Lynchburg, 1867.

Featherstonhaugh, George, *Excursion Through the Slave States.* London, 1844.

Fishwick, Marshall, *Lee after the War.* New York, 1963.

Fisk and Hatch, *Prospectuses on the Chesapeake and Ohio Railroad and the Chesapeake and Ohio Railway.* New York, 1868–1887.

Fitch, William Edward, *Mineral Waters of the United States and American Spas.* Philadelphia, 1927.

Freeman, Douglas Southall, *R. E. Lee.* New York, 1934–1935.

Furnas, J.C., *The Life and Times of the Late Demon Rum.* New York, 1965.

Gibson, Charles Dana, *The Gibson Book.* New York, 1906.

Goldman, Eric F., *Charles J. Bonaparte, Patrician Reformer.* Baltimore, 1943.

[Hagner, Mary M.] *Mark Pencil, The White Sulphur Papers, or Life at the Springs of Western Virginia.* New York, 1839.

Hayem, Georges, *Physical and Natural Therapeutics.* Philadelphia, 1895.

Hepburn, Andrew, *The Great Resorts of North America.* New York, 1965.

Horner, William E., *Observations on the Mineral Waters of the Southwestern Part of Virginia.* Philadelphia, 1834.

Howe, Henry, *Historical Collections of Virginia.* Charleston, S. C., 1845.

Ingalls, Fay, *The Valley Road.* Cleveland, 1949.

James, Marquis, *Andrew Jackson.* Indianapolis, 1933–1937.

Kennedy, John P., *Swallow Barn, or a Sojourn in the Old Dominion.* Philadelphia, 1832.

Kimmel, Stanley Preston, *The Mad Booths of Maryland.* Indianapolis, 1940.

Lee, R. E., Jr., *Recollections of R. E. Lee.* New York, 1893.

Ludy, Robert B., *Historic Hotels of the World, Past and Present.* Philadelphia, 1927.

Martineau, Harriet, *Society in America.*

McAllister, J.T., *Historical Sketches of Virginia Hot Springs, Warm Sulphur Springs and Bath County, Virginia.* Hot Springs, 1908.

Macartney, Clarence Edward, and Dorrance Gordon, *The Bonapartes in America.* Philadelphia, 1939.

MacCorkle, William Alexander, *White Sulphur Springs*. New York, 1916.

MacPherson, John, *The Baths and Wells of Europe*. London, 1869.

Metcalfe, Richard, *The Rise and Progress of Hydropathy in England and Scotland*. London, 1912.

Moorman, John J., *A Directory for the Use of the White Sulphur Waters*. Philadelphia, 1839. This pamphlet was expanded into book form, and went through many editions until the year 1873.

National Cyclopaedia of American Biography. New York, 1892–1965.

[Nicklin, Philip Houlbrooke], *Peregrine Prolix, Letters from the Virginia Springs*. New York, 1835, 1837, 1845.

North, M. L., *Saratoga Waters, or the Invalid at Saratoga*. New York, 1843.

Palmer, Frederick, *John J. Pershing, General of the Armies*. Harrisburg, 1948.

Parton, James, *Life of Andrew Jackson*. New York, 1860.

Perkins, T. H., *The Springs of Virginia*. Boston, 1839.

Pershing, John Joseph, *My Experiences in the World War*. New York, 1931.

Price, Paul H., and Heck, E. T., *Greenbrier County*. Wheeling, 1939.

Price, Paul H., McCue, J. B., and Hoskins, Homer A., *Springs of West Virginia*. Morgantown, 1936.

Reniers, Perceval, *The Springs of Virginia*. Chapel Hill, 1941.

Rhodes, Harrison, *In Vacation America*. New York, 1915.

Riley, Franklin, *General Robert E. Lee after Appomattox*. New York, 1922.

Rouelle, John, *A Complete Treatise on the Mineral Waters of Virginia*. Philadelphia, 1792.

Seager, Robert, *And Tyler, Too*. New York, 1961.

Selden, John, *White Sulphur Springs* (drama). Washington, 1901.

Smith, James Reuel, *Springs and Wells of Manhattan and the Bronx*. New York, 1938.

Snead, Sam[uel Jackson], and Stump, Al [J.], *Education of a Golfer*. New York, 1962.

Steel, John H., *An Analysis of the Congress Spring*. New York, 1856.

Sullivan, Mark, *Our Times*. New York, 1926–1935.

Tanner, Henry, *The American Traveller*. Philadelphia, 1834.

Taylor, Quintard, *White Sulphur Springs Since 1778*.

Taylor, Walter H., *Four Years with General Lee*. New York, 1878.

Taylor, Walter H., *General Lee*. Norfolk, 1906.

Turner, Charles Wilson, *Chessie's Road*. Richmond, 1956.

Tyler, Lyon Gardiner, *The Letters and Times of the Tylers*. Richmond, 1884–1896.

Walton, George Edward, *Mineral Springs of the United States and Canada*. New York, 1873.

The War of the Rebellion, Official Records of the Union and Confederate Armies. Washington, 1880–1901

Williams, T. Harry, *P. G. T. Beauregard, Napoleon in Gray*. Baton Rouge, 1955.

Willoughby, Lois, *History of Greenbrier County*.

Wilson, [Thomas] Woodrow, *R. E. Lee, an Interpretation*. Chapel Hill, 1924.

Windsor, Edward, Duke of, *A King's Story*. New York, 1951.

Windsor, Wallis Warfield, *The Heart Has Its Reasons*. New York, 1956.

Published by
Arndt, Preston, Chapin, Lamb & Keen, Inc.
Printed in the Netherlands
by Joh. Enschedé en Zonen, Haarlem